Philips Family
AND THE Early Church

Joy Haney

Cover art work by Nick LeGuern.

Philip's Family and the Early Church by Joy Haney
Published by Radiant Life Publications
©1993

Printed in the United States of America.

ISBN 1-880969-12-2

Introduction

This book is based on true and historical information. Much research has been done to unearth interesting but unfamiliar stories and facts that will help bring the reader to a better understanding of the beginning of the Church that Jesus Christ founded.

The events in the Book of Acts will be looked at through the eyes of Philip, the Evangelist, his family, and other believers. The author's imagination concerning conversations, feelings, and domestic activities could be true, but are not scripturally documented such as romantic feelings one of Philip's daughters has toward Stephen, the martyr.

We know that Philip had a wife, but it is thought that she died and left him a widower with four daughters. The author uses her imagination to depict what could have been, but all stories and activities of the Early Church presented in this book are true based on the Holy Bible, commentaries, and historical accounts. Read this book and then read the Book of Acts in the King James Version of the Holy Bible, and you will discover what the Early Church preached and practiced and will feel the fire that was their daily companion.

Philip first lived around Jerusalem, for he was one of the original seven that took care of the daily ministrations of the widows. When persecution broke out, he first went to Samaria and other places to minister and then settled in Caesarea with his four daughters who were prophetesses. Their whole family was full of zeal and love towards Jesus and their home was a meeting place for new believers to come together.

Although there are suppositions about feelings, thoughts, and happenings that surround the facts, the basic message of the book is built on truth, and that is the desire of the author: to awaken the reader to the truth of the Early Church, the original method

of baptism, the infilling of the Holy Ghost and the fire of each believer.

Foreword

An open letter to the author from Rev. David F. Gray, D.D., pastor, author, speaker, and Bible theologian and teacher:

Dear Joy,

I have just finished reading *Philip's Family and the Early Church*.   Even though you called it a "rough draft," I must say that it was an exhilarating experience.

The characters in the book of Acts stepped out of the misty past and became living flesh-and-blood individuals.   An inspired touch was your use of events from secular history which, when woven into the Biblical narrative, made it live with genuine fascination and intrigue. The story was altogether charming as well as factual and true to the inspired account. I truly felt that I was transported into the first century and became part of the lives of the Bible characters.

Altogether it was a fun and exciting read. The human emotions woven into the fast-moving events made the story exciting.

Thanks for letting me walk with you into the lives of these Bible characters.

In Him,
David F. Gray

Preface

At the time of the death of Jesus, Jerusalem was a major city. Its status as the center of religious life for the Jews dated back a thousand years to King David, who had captured the Jebusite citadel of Zion and rebuilt it as the "City of David."

In the time of the early Christian movement, Jerusalem was a lively city: its narrow, steeply pitched streets were crowded with bazaars, and during festival seasons were thronged with foreign pilgrims and grumpy caravan animals. At the heart of everything was the Temple. A magnificent structure, it was the third to be erected on this site. The first was Solomon's until the Babylonians destroyed it. A replacement was started during the reign of the Persian King, Cyrus the Great. When King Herod the Great took power, he tore down the second temple and started a new one, about 20 B.C. This became the centerpiece for other buildings, which included three monumental towers, his own gigantic palace, and a huge fortress, the Antonia, which housed the Roman garrison. In addition he expanded the water-supply system.

Almost all of Jerusalem's population was engaged in one way or another in the work of the Temple—as craftsmen providing and repairing necessary ritual objects, incense makers, dealers in sacrificial animals, providers for the pilgrims such as innkeepers and proprietors of restaurants, scholars and priests. There were moneychangers and bankers; virtually all people deposited their money there.

The wealthiest Jews in Jerusalem were the great land proprietors, officials in the Roman tax system and the priestly aristocracy. These groups tended to identify more with the values of the Greek and Roman upper classes. For them there was a Greek-style theater, a sports stadium, and many fine homes on the western hill of the Upper City.

To the Romans, Jerusalem was important largely as a good source of revenue. An appointed governor, who resided in Caesarea, was in charge of the province that included Jerusalem. Many of Jerusalem's markets catered mainly to the pilgrim trade. Pilgrims sometimes far outnumbered the local population, so trade could be intense with haggling over prices and quality. Shops opened just after dawn, and most business was conducted during the day. Jumbled close together, the shops offered items of every description—fabrics, garments, pottery, glassware, brass and copper ware, jewelry, perfumes, spices, household articles, fruits and vegetables. They were crowded, noisy and exciting. People often gathered to the market places to exchange salutations and news.

Chapter 1

As the Judean sun rose upon the family homes nestled in the hills that surrounded Jerusalem, the holy city, the air seemed to breathe anticipation of things to come. The Roman army grew larger and the influence of the Greeks was abounding while a certain religious group was entering into new and unmarked areas.

As the dawn caressed the hills with its cooling touch, Philip, one of the believers in Christ, was kissing his wife goodbye for the day. She sensed his repressed excitement as he told her he was joining other believers for some more instructions from the Christ. "There is something about to happen that will change our world. I feel it deep within me," he said as he walked from the house into the courtyard.

As she heard those startling words, she pondered over the days that had been. The agonizing days that had led to the crucifixion of Jesus and the awful chant of the crowd seemed to swell in her mind as she remembered the senselessness of it all. The frown on her face broke into a smile when she thought of the miraculous resurrection of Christ. Even now the neighbors still talked about the phenomenon.

As Philip made his way to the Mount of Olives near Bethany, a Sabbath Day's journey from the city, he was joined by other believers who were on the same journey. As they finally approached the foot of the mountain, they saw quite a large group of people gathered there looking up towards the high point of the Mount of Olives, which stood 2,641 feet above the Mediterranean Sea.

As their eyes focused upon Jesus, the object of everyone's attention, there seemed to be a special light about him. When he began to speak, the milling, talking crowd hushed in reverent silence, sensing the importance of the meeting. He instructed them to go to Jerusalem and wait for the promise from the Father. He said, "John baptized you with water, but ye shall be baptized with the Holy Ghost not many days hence." As they gazed steadfastly at Jesus as he gave his final instructions to them, they noticed his feet were no longer on the ground. They were spellbound with wonder and awe as He floated higher and higher until He was enveloped in a cloud and eventually disappeared.

As they continued to gaze at the vacant sky where once He had been, suddenly two angels in shiny apparel appeared and gave them hope saying, "This same Jesus which is taken up from you shall so come in like manner as ye have seen him go into heaven."

As Philip listened he stored it in his memory, "Jesus is coming back again!"

As the leaders discussed among themselves what to do, it was decided that everyone should meet at a certain upper room in Jerusalem to literally wait for the promise that Jesus said would be sent.

Philip turned to his friends and told them he was going home to tell his wife about the strange instructions. Upon leaving he assured them, "As soon as I go home and tell my family, I will meet you there."

Philip's steps homeward along the dusty road were with purpose and hurried excitement. As he joyously approached his house, the door was flung open by his wife as she ran into the courtyard with their four girls following her, awaiting his arrival.

"Oh, Darling," he said as he embraced her, "strange things have happened today. Jesus, the one we have followed, has ascended into heaven up into the clouds. I saw it with my own eyes. After he disappeared, two angels appeared and told us he was coming back again. But before Jesus left, he told us to go and tarry at Jerusalem and wait for the promise of the Father. The angels told us that we would be baptized with the Holy Ghost."

"Philip!" she cried, "It sounds like a fairy tale or one of the stories told by the Greeks. What will we do? The Feast of the Weeks is ten days away. Will you stay there all that time? Should the girls and I come then with our neighbors and friends? What should we do?"

Philip calmed his wife by saying, "I have thought it all out on the way home. I am going back to wait at Jerusalem with the others in the upper room. Because of the children you will come when everyone comes for the celebration. You can come with my uncle's family. He will help you bring everything that is needed. The girls can help you prepare everything for the festival."

Joy Haney

Philip paused and then cried, "Oh, Darling, if you could have seen his eyes! It was the most phenomenal thing I have ever experienced. Can you imagine talking with someone and then see him disappear up beyond the clouds? It sounds unbelievable, but it happened! My body is tingling with feverish excitement, and I cannot wait to go to Jerusalem and see what this Holy Ghost is that is going to be poured out upon us!"

He looked at his four daughters, Charitine, Irais, Hermoine, and Eutychiane and told them, "I feel very deeply that you four girls are going to be a part of this infilling that is soon to take place. May God be with you as I go. You be sure to help your mother. You know she has been having fainting spells lately. She is not strong. You must lighten her load as you prepare for the celebration."

He then gathered his things, kissed his family goodbye, made final arrangements where to meet him and then with a final wave of his hand was gone into the night towards a destination that would alter the course of his life. Philip could sense something different taking place, but he could not know the transformation that was soon to transpire. He would be changed forever.

As he entered the city and walked down the narrow cobblestone streets lit only by dim lights, the night sounds had already begun. When he entered the lower courtyard of the upper room where his friends and other believers were already starting to gather, the night sounds were mixed with a sound coming from upstairs. There were voices speaking and praying with urgency and joy. As Philip quickly climbed the stairs going towards the entrance of the meeting place someone opened the door and peered out into the night.

"Oh Philip, it is you. We wondered who was coming up the stairs."

Philip looked around at the large group and asked his friend, "How many do you think are here?"

"There seems to be about 120 present now. They have been coming in all evening. Peter has been talking to us telling us what to do and how to pray," Stephen replied.

As the 120 Jews joined in prayer and worship waiting for the promise, there came an unshakable belief that it was coming soon. The next few days were filled with monumental happenings. Simon Peter, feeling a special unction, stood up and began to speak with earnestness. He told them about the

Joy Haney

original twelve and how one of them, Judas Iscariot, had failed. "We need to appoint someone to take his place," he said.

He then called the ten to join him up front: James, John, Andrew, Philip, Thomas, Bartholomew, Matthew, James, the son of Alphaeas, Simon Zelotes and Judas, the brother of James. There were two men appointed to be chosen: Joseph, who was called Barsabas and surnamed Justus, and Matthias. Then in reverence they prayed, "Lord, you know the hearts of all men. Show which of these two you have chosen to take part of this ministry and apostleship from which Judas by transgression fell." Then they cast lots and the lot fell upon Matthias. So the twelve were complete again.

For ten long days, both men and women, including Mary, the mother of Jesus, prayed and waited for the outpouring of the Holy Ghost.

Chapter 2

While the 120 were closely clustered together in the upper room, there was a stir taking place outside their four walls. Jews from surrounding areas were traveling to Jerusalem for the great celebration of the Feast of Weeks. Caravans streamed into the city. They were coming from North Africa, from Asia Minor, from Rome and from the Arab countries as well. Camels, horses, and mules traveled side by side as the devout Jewish people made their way for another important celebration. It was nearing the fiftieth day after the barley harvest celebration of Passover.

Soon after midnight the temple gates were opened that offerings for the day might be examined by the priests. At sunrise occurred the regular daily sacrifice, and soon afterwards the festal offerings. Amid singing of the "Hallel," the ceremonies of Pentecost began. The two lambs were first waved alive; then after their sacrifice, the breast and shoulder were laid beside the two loaves of bread that had been prepared and baked the day before. Then followed the other appointed sacrifices and the free-will gifts. The rest of the day was spent in festive gatherings to which the poor, the stranger, and the Levite were invited.

Philip's family and neighbors were among the great multitudes that thronged toward Jerusalem. The weariness and labor of the seven weeks' harvest was forgotten. This was celebration day. Charitine asked her sister, "Do you think Stephen will be there?"

Irais innocently replied with devilishment dancing in her dark, sparkling eyes, "Why do you ask?"

Charitine tried to answer in an offhand manner, "Oh, I was just wondering."

Hermoine exclaimed, "Just wondering? Do you think we do not see the way you look at Stephen and hear the way you say his name?"

Joy Haney

Their mother interrupted this conversation with, "Girls, I don't know if I can make the journey. The pain around my heart is increasing."

"Oh, mother," they cried, "you ride the donkey. We will carry the things that he carries on his back."

As they helped their mother onto the donkey, their thoughts grew more sober. What would they do if something happened to their dear mother? The pain in her chest seemed to be increasing more and more.

If they could have seen into the future and the pain that awaited them, they would have not have enjoyed the rest of the trip nor the days ahead.

As they neared the city, it seemed their mother was feeling better. In an atmosphere of congeniality, neighbor talked with neighbor, and they began to chatter happily again in anticipation of the forthcoming festivities and reunion with their father. It was difficult to make progress into the city as thousands of people were entering at the same time. Moving at a snail's pace, calling greetings to friends, they finally arrived at the appointed place of the feast. Looking around they did not see Philip who was to meet them there.

As the day wore on and the festivities were in full swing, there came a man into their area with news that shook their traditional observance. He passionately told them, "There is a group of men and women who are gathered together and they are speaking in many different languages. Not only are they speaking in many tongues, but there was a great sound that came into the area where they were and it sounded like a mighty rushing wind."

The crowd started asking questions. "Where are they?" "What tongues are they speaking in?" "What are they saying?"

The messenger said, "People from many nations who have come for the feast are astonished to hear them speak in their language. They are talking in a language foreign to themselves but understood by the Medes, Asians, Egyptians, Arabs, and many others. They are all talking about the wonderful works of God."

"Take us to this great thing!" the people cried.

Philip's family pressed close to the messenger as he led them through the crowded streets to the area of the upper room. When they came near the 120 speaking in tongues, they could see that something great had happened and were amazed, as were others. They could see Philip, but he was in another dimension. His hands were raised in worship to God

Joy Haney

and they heard him speak with a language they had never heard him speak before.

One of the crowd shouted, "These men are drunk!"

People were in shock, pushing and trying to get closer to this thing that had never happened before. As they all were talking and asking questions, Peter stood up and the eleven apostles stood with him. He lifted his voice and said, "These are not drunk, as you suppose, seeing it is but the third hour of the day. This is that which was spoken by Joel, the prophet: In the last days, says God, I will pour out of my Spirit upon all flesh: and your sons and daughters shall prophesy. Men and brothers, let me freely speak to you of the patriarch David, that he being a prophet spoke of Christ. God has raised up this Jesus, whereof we all are witnesses. He has ascended into heaven, and having received of the Father the promise of the Holy Ghost, he has poured it out today. That is what you see and hear. Therefore, let all the house of Israel know, that God has made that same Jesus, whom you have crucified, both Lord and Christ."

Peter paused and looked with piercing eyes at all the people. Many of them were moved in their spirit and passionately cried, "What must we do to be saved?"

Peter again thundered forth the way of salvation. "Repent, and be baptized every one of you in the name of Jesus Christ for the remission of sins, and you shall receive the gift of the Holy Ghost. For this promise is to you and to your children and to all that are afar off, even as many as the Lord our God shall call." Peter ended his message with, "Save yourselves from this untoward generation!"

Word spread like wildfire through the streets of Jerusalem into every house and place of festivity, even into the temple. People quickly pressed into the courtyard and the upper room until there were 3,000 people receiving the Holy Ghost and being baptized, including Philip's family.

"There never was a Pentecost like this Pentecost," wrote one Jewish grandmother in her daily journal.

Chapter 3

It was a different family that made its way home after the festivities of the Feast of Weeks. The Day of Pentecost changed everything. Philip talked with his wife and daughters as they approached their house. He asked them, "Do you feel any different?"

"Father," Hermoine spoke for them all, "it is the most wonderful experience we have ever had. I feel like a glow is inside of me as if there was a fire burning brightly in my heart." The other girls nodded in assent.

As they walked happily on, Philip saw a new glow in his wife's face. He remarked about it. "Honey, your face is shining. I've never seen you so happy."

She replied, "Do you remember the prophets of old talking about the 'rest' that would be given with the stammering of tongues? Well, today I had stammering lips and then I spoke the most beautiful language. The most glorious peace and joy filled my whole being."

Philip pressed his wife's hand and said, "Oh, Darling, it is wonderful, isn't it? You do not know how good it makes me feel to see you glowing so!"

"Philip," she responded, "I feel strange. Almost like I am going to be leaving you and the family, but now I have hope. Do you remember how Jesus told the multitude while he was on earth that the Holy Ghost would be a comforter? Well, if anything should happen to me—you will have a divine comforter. You know I have had a weak heart for a long time now but, Husband, do not despair when my time comes to go. The girls will take good care of you, and somehow I feel like God has a special place in his kingdom for you."

"Oh, Darling! Do not speak of your departing on our most happy day! This is no time to be sad, but to rejoice." Philip continued, "Even as you spoke about that special place in the kingdom, somehow that feeling came over me today while I was receiving the Holy Spirit in Jerusalem."

"Philip, it is coming. I know it is coming. You will have a unique responsibility in this new Church," she said as she nodded her head vigorously.

As they came abreast of the courtyard of their home they all paused and looked up at the star-studded sky and whispered a silent prayer for the beautiful Day of Pentecost that had been theirs. Then they said "Good night" to their fellow travelers and relatives following along behind, thanking them for the use of their donkey and their help in the preparation of the Feast of Weeks. They then entered the courtyard and went into the house.

Early the next morning Philip awakened suddenly from sleep with a strange feeling inside of him. He walked outside and looked at the fading morning star, but could not shake the feeling that something was amiss. He silently went back inside the house, checked to make sure the lamp had enough oil to burn for awhile longer, then made his way over to the bed where his wife slept.

As he glanced down at her he noticed her face had a transparency about it that had never been there before. He remembered the words that she had spoken last night—words that had grabbed at his heart—and then he knew. His wife was gone. She would be his dear companion no more. That part of his life was over. As he knelt by the bed and took her cold hand, tears of grief gushed forth from his eyes, overflowing from his breaking heart. He cried aloud for what was taken from him. "Oh, God," he prayed, "send that comforter my wife talked about last night. Console me in this dark hour."

As sobs racked his body, he felt a comforting presence enter the room—one he had never felt before. He knew the Holy Spirit was ministering to the deep hurts within him.

Days later, after the funeral and after the relatives one by one went back to their normal routine, things returned to a more normal schedule. The difference was, life would never be normal again. It was not only the death of his wife. It was the new experience he received on the Day of Pentecost. Ever since that day there had been a glow inside of him. He had a new fire that made him want to tell others about it.

It became a common sight to see Philip spend more and more of his time going to the temple and conversing with other Jews about this new religion that had sprung up after Christ's ascension. It was still the talk in the marketplaces, in the temple courtyard and among all his friends.

The Apostles organized daily prayer meetings and many people attended them faithfully. Not only were the people praying and teaching the Scriptures to those that were interested, there were great miracles taking place.

Philip arrived home one evening and was welcomed by a very excited group of young ladies. "Father, is it true? We heard there were 5,000 new believers added to the new church. We also heard that a lame man was healed at Gate Beautiful. Is it true?"

Philip looked at their happy, flushed faces that reflected their hard work in the kitchen, garden and household and replied, "Yes, it is true. The lame man was healed at Gate Beautiful and 5,000 new believers have joined the followers of Jesus Christ, but with truth comes trouble."

"What do you mean, Father?" asked Irais.

"Today the priests, Sadducees, and the captain of the temple arrested Peter and John and put them in jail overnight. It does not look good, my daughters. Let us pray this night for the leaders of our new found faith, that God would be with them."

The next morning Philip told his daughters that he was attending a special meeting to be held that day. He told them not to worry about him, that he would be gone all day.

Philip approached the meeting with gladness and suppressed excitement. He reflected that this Holy Spirit within him was still powerful and glowing and often when he prayed he would speak in tongues all over again. When he arrived at the meeting he saw that it was already in progress.

Peter was telling everyone what had happened. He said, "Can you imagine? Annas, the high priest and Caiaphas were there and all their relatives. They surrounded us and asked us by what power we had done this miracle of the lame man being healed. We told them that it had been done by the name of Jesus Christ of Nazareth, whom they had crucified, and that there was none other name under heaven whereby men could be saved."

Nicanor, one of the believers, asked in amazement, "What was their response?"

John answered, "They commanded us not to teach or speak in the name of Jesus ever again."

Nicolas asked, "What did you tell them?"

Peter said, "We asked them, 'Is it right for us to hearken unto you or unto God?' Then we told them we could only speak of the things which we had seen or heard."

When the company of believers at the meeting heard these words they lifted up their voices and prayed, "Lord, you are God which has made heaven and earth and the sea and all that is in them. Behold, Lord, their threatenings and grant unto your servants boldness to speak your word by stretching forth your hand to heal and that signs and wonders may be done by your holy child Jesus."

Suddenly as they were all praying, the meeting place was literally shaken by the power of God and they were filled with the Holy Ghost all over again!

When Philip finally returned home that night it was with a heart rejoicing that the Spirit of God was with the new believers so mightily. As he reflected about the attitude of the priests, he wondered why they were having such a hard time receiving truth— that Jesus Christ was Lord, that he had come to bring grace and to fulfill the law, and that because He was the supreme sacrifice they did not have to offer sacrifices anymore. Instead of rolling sins ahead for a year, Christ had made it possible to be instantly forgiven. He was the Saviour of the world! Why couldn't all the Jews see it?

Again when he entered the door of his house, his four daughters wanted to know all that had happened. He talked between bites as he ate the delicious meal they had prepared for him. Their eyes were shining as they listened to the excitement that this new doctrine was creating among the leaders of the old religion. When he finished eating he asked, "How would you girls like to go into the City with me tomorrow? You could get a feeling of the excitement that is abounding and pick up the things you need at the market while we are there."

They all four grabbed their father, kissed him and thanked him, not being able to contain their enthusiasm over tomorrow's venture.

The next morning, after rising early, completing the chores, and eating breakfast, the five of them started off to the City. As they approached the gates they saw several people carrying beds in which sick people lay. One mother was bringing a daughter who was vexed with an evil spirit.

Philip asked them where they were headed, and several answered at once. "We are going to Solomon's porch."

"What is happening there?"

"Many people are being healed, so we are bringing our family members to be healed."

Hermoine, who had studied medicine, asked, "Oh, Father, let us go to Solomon's porch, please."

So they went. But when they got close, there were so many people thronging the temple area that there was not room for everyone on the porch. People were laying the sick right in the street on beds and couches hoping that the shadow of Peter might fall on them and that they would be healed.

It was exhilarating, joyous and glorious. People that had been sick for years were jumping off couches and beds, running around praising God. Men were embracing wives that had been sick unto death, but who were now healed. Everyone that came into the area was healed instantly. There was great singing, dancing, shouting and celebration until suddenly the high priest and his company rose up with indignation, and went storming into the temple area. There they found the Apostles preaching to the people about Jesus, and praying for the sick in the Name of Jesus. As they watched the sick ones being healed, so furious was their anger over this new display of power, that they arrested the Apostles and put them in prison.

They then turned to the crowd and told them to disperse and go home. Philip and his daughters, who had been joyously singing, became subdued when they realized that this new doctrine of Christ

Jesus was not welcome in the old established religious circles.

Philip led his family away from Solomon's porch area down to the marketplace where the girls purchased a few needed items. Then they all started for home praising God, but with concern about the future.

Joy Haney

Chapter 4

The next day Philip and the girls all stayed home doing chores that needed to be done. In their morning devotions they prayed fervently for the safety of the Apostles.

Around noon, Parmenas, their father's friend and a believer, walked into the courtyard and the girls welcomed him eagerly as Charitine ran to call her father. Hermoine told Parmenas, "You are just in time for lunch. You must stay and eat with us."

When all were seated at the table, Parmenas said, "I've brought news, my friends. I was in the City this morning and found that something unbelievable happened last night."

"What happened?" they asked in unison.

"Last night an angel of the Lord came and opened the prison doors and told the Apostles to go stand and speak in the temple to the people all the words of life. Then he disappeared. The disciples came back early this morning and were teaching in the temple when the high priest and his company came and arrested them again.

"Well," continued Parmenas, "Peter preached to them and they got so mad that they were going to kill them but Gamaliel cooled them down and said, 'If it is of God you cannot fight it, but if it is of man it will fall anyway, so give it some time.' Instead of killing them, they beat them and told them to never speak the name of Jesus again."

Philip said, "That will not stop them or the Church. There is power and faith growing in every believer's heart. I predict that soon many believers will be doing miracles, signs, and wonders. This thing is going to grow and spread until other cities and countries will also hear this gospel and witness the power of Jesus Christ."

Charitine asked with shining eyes, "Father, do you think this new power that we have in us will enable us to teach others about Christ also?"

"Oh, yes, my daughter! All of you and most believers are already alive with new zeal. As you learn more, you will teach and people will be converted. It is sooner than we think."

As they finished their meal, Parmenas said his thanks for the food and hospitality and embraced Philip before leaving. He turned before walking out the door and said, "Oh, yes, next Thursday there is a special meeting called for all the believers. I know you will want to be there."

"I'll be there. Good day to you, Parmenas," said Philip.

On Thursday, the day of the meeting, Philip left early in the morning with some of his friends. As they walked towards the City, Stephen asked, "What do you think this meeting is about?"

"It is probably to do with the rapid spread of the Apostle's doctrine and all that has been happening lately," volunteered Philip.

"One thing I know," said Stephen, "I've never felt so alive before in all my life. This is the greatest thing that ever happened to me."

All the men traveling together voiced the same sentiment while Nicolas said, "I feel like I'm chomping at the bit like my old horse does when he wants to race. I am ready for action. I have been studying with the Apostles and now I want to help others find what we have found."

They were all nodding their heads in assent as they neared the City and the place of the meeting. There were already hundreds there and as they made their way near to where the Apostles were standing, Peter raised his voice and said, "This meeting was called for a special need among us. You know that persecution has arisen from the old religious order and that we have been imprisoned twice. We also were beaten because of the priest's anger against us. Now we have another problem. You understand that one of the church's first functions is to care for the widows that have embraced the Christian faith. There have been murmurings against us saying that we have neglected the Grecian widows. It is not in our heart to do so, but the work load of the propagation of the gospel is taking up all of our time. We have decided to choose seven men among this group here today who are honest, full of the Holy Ghost and faith and wisdom that can take care of this business. We then can give ourselves full-time to prayer and ministry of the Word to others."

When Peter finished speaking, approval was voiced throughout the crowd. It did not take long for the seven to be chosen. They were already leaders and men of renown who had been filled with the Spirit of God. John then read the names chosen and asked them to step forward for prayer: Philip, Prochorus, Nicanor, Timon, Parmenas, Stephen and Nicolas. The Apostles laid hands on them and prayed for them, sending them forth to work in their new position.

After the meting was over Philip asked the other six to come to his house the following day to make preparations for their new responsibility. They all agreed and departed each to his own home after visiting awhile with other disciples of the Lord Jesus.

The next day the four daughters scrubbed the house, baked bread and pastries and prepared everything for the evening's meeting. Charitine was especially glowing. "Isn't it wonderful? Stephen is coming to our house tonight."

"What about the others?" Irais gently reminded her.

"Oh yes, but Stephen is so handsome and big," Charitine said dreamily.

"You're always thinking about Stephen," scolded Eutychiane.

"Well, when you are in love that isn't hard," Charitine argued back.

"Does father know about this?" asked Hermoine.

"No, and don't you tell him," Charitine spoke with feeling.

"Hush! Here he comes now," whispered Irais.

"Well, well, how's my four beautiful hard-working daughters?" Philip asked when he entered the house.

"Father, we are all excited about tonight! Everything is ready and we are just putting finishing touches on things," Hermoine responded. "I know it will be a great meeting."

As evening shadows darkened the mountains of Judea, one lone figure, Stephen, walked quickly along the road from the west of the city where the Judean highlands slope down to meet the lowland. He was on his way to an important meeting with "The Seven," as they were called.

He was thinking of his recent appointment as he approached the palatial home of Philip, when his thoughts were interrupted by a familiar voice.

"Stephen, it is good to see you," spoke Nicanor with joy. The two men embraced and continued on together arriving at the well-lit home where the door was thrown open by a beautiful young lady. Charitine greeted the two men warmly while ushering them into the courtyard where the others were waiting. Stephen glancing around smiled and shook hands with the other five who made up the Seven.

Philip then led them up the narrow stairs which led to the flat rooftop where the meeting was being held. He then called it to order and requested Timon to pray before beginning.

Timon lifted his hands toward heaven in Jewish fashion and prayed eloquently, "Oh, Lord God of the heavens, who stretches them out like a curtain and sits upon the circle of the earth, we ask your holy blessing upon us this night. We intreat the God that delivered Moses and our forefathers from the hand of the enemy, to help us. Give us insight and direction from above as we seek to do your will. Amen!"

As Timon finished praying, Philip called upon Stephen to proceed with the evening's meeting concerning the appointment by the Apostles. The very atmosphere pulsated with zeal, warmth, and enthusiasm. Stephen, with vibrant fire and love flowing from him, stood with outstretched hands saying, "Brethren, we have been chosen to do a great work. We have been filled with the Spirit the Messiah promised would descend upon us and now we will work the works he instructed us to do."

Downstairs, Charitine whispered to Irais, "Isn't he handsome? I feel like my heart is going to burst with my love for him."

"Does he know?" questioned Irais.

"He looked at me in a special way when I met him and Nicanor at the door tonight."

Hermoine, the more thoughtful sister, asked, "What would father say if he knew? You know how fastidious he is about rituals, traditions, and customs."

"Oh, I think it is so romantic," little Eutychiane breathlessly sighed.

"You are too young to know about romance, Eutychiane," said Charitine sternly, then smiled indulgently at her younger sister.

The four girls went to the bottom of the stairs and heard the men talking about Grecian widows, synagogues, and other significant matters. Hermoine, the oldest, felt a shiver of fear run through her. So much had happened since the crucifixion of Jesus, the Messiah.

She remembered the days following the crucifixion. There was the upper room experience that all the Jews were talking about. She still could not understand the fire that had rested upon everyone's head, but it had transformed everyone that had experienced it. Peter and John had performed a miracle at the Gate Beautiful and all her friends were astounded. It was just unbelievable! Her thoughts leaped to the death of Ananias and Sapphira. They had lied to the Holy Ghost and when Peter revealed it they both fell dead. Since then persecution had started against the followers of Christ and some of the Apostles had been beaten and thrown in jail.

As Hermoine listened to traces of conversation floating down the stairs and looked at her three beautiful dark-eyed sisters, she wondered where it would all lead to and what else would happen.

Later in the evening, the Seven came down the stairs and partook of the delicious refreshments. One could not help but sense the electricity that seemed to flow between Stephen and Charitine.

As the men finally left, Charitine mooned about the house preparing for the night, dreaming of flashing dark eyes and dark wavy hair belonging to one called Stephen.

Chapter 5

The days following found not only the Apostles doing miracles and teaching the people, but now the Seven, as well as many other disciples, became powerful in the Spirit. So great was their zeal that numbers were added daily to the Church and even a great company of priests were converted to the new faith.

Stephen became one of the leading figures full of faith and power and did many wonders and miracles, so much that the synagogue of the Libertines, Cyrenians, and Alexandrians as well as others began to dispute with Stephen.

He told them that the coming of Jesus of Nazareth rendered the Temple and its sacrifices—

the glory of Jerusalem—unnecessary. These were fighting words indeed!

The men that disputed with him did not have any power against the wisdom and the spirit in which he spoke. They were baffled and disturbed by this new enemy against whom they could not win. So they instigated a demonstration against Stephen and told some of the people to lie and say they had heard him blaspheme against God.

They became so angry that they took hold of him and brought him to the Council of the High Priest at the Sanhedrin, which was the highest court of justice and the supreme council at Jerusalem. The decisions of the Sanhedrin were of inviolable force, and were binding upon all teachers of the Law and all judges. The meetings were held from the time of the offering of the daily morning sacrifice until that of the evening sacrifice except on Sabbath and feast days.

As Stephen stood before them his face shown like an angel. The council was shocked and the high priest asked him, "Is this true which they have said?"

Stephen glanced around at all the people and then began to speak. "Men and brethren, the God of Abraham appeared to Abraham and told him to get out of his country and come into a land that he would show him. Abraham obeyed the Lord and

Joy Haney

God promised him a child which he gave him. Isaac was born and he begat Jacob and Jacob begat the twelve patriarchs.

"The patriarchs were envious of Joseph and sold him into Egypt but God was with him. He delivered Joseph out of all his afflictions and when famine came to Egypt, God caused Joseph to be the ruler under Pharaoh over the food stored. Joseph died and another ruler arose that knew not Joseph. Then Moses was born and God raised him up to deliver the children of Israel out of Egyptian rule. They were brought forth but time after time they forgot God and refused to worship him. Into this David was raised up to be king and then Solomon, who built a temple for the Lord.

"But the Most High dwells not in temples made with hands. He seeks to dwell in the heart of men!"

Then Stephen looked all the priests square in the eye and said, "You stiff-necked and uncircumcised in heart and ears. You always resist the Holy Ghost just as your fathers did."

The company of priests became so angry that they rushed at Stephen and tried to bite him with their teeth. But Stephen just looked up into the heavens and saw a vision and told them what he saw. He said, "I see the Son of man standing on the right hand of God."

This angered them so much that they stopped up their ears, grabbed him by the arms, picked him up, led him to the outskirts of the city and flung him away from them. Then they started stoning him.

When the rocks started flying and Stephen felt the pain of the impact against his skin, he cried, "Lord Jesus, receive my spirit." He then kneeled down and asked God to forgive his accusers. Standing close by was a young man named Saul who guarded the stoners' coats.

Hermoine had gone into the city with Philip the following day and news of the stoning was on the lips of all the followers of Christ. It was being talked about in the streets, inns, temple, marketplace—it was discussed everywhere.

"Father, this is horrible!" cried Hermoine. "This is going to be terrible for Charitine."

Philip's ears perked up, "It is horrible, but why for Charitine?"

"Oh, Father, that is all she has been talking about lately—Stephen this, Stephen that. Her heart is going to be broken."

Joy Haney

Philip pondered this and tried to think how to break the news to the girls when he arrived home. "First their mother, now a close friend of the family," he thought.

Later that night after dinner, Philip gathered his family around him. "Girls, I want to talk to you," he began. "These are days of unrest. Since the outpouring of the Spirit on the day of Pentecost there has been a growing resentment among the religious leaders here in Jerusalem against it. There has been persecution, but it is increasing. I feel like it is going to gain momentum and it will reach into Rome and other places. Whatever happens, we must be strong, for Jesus talked about being hated for his name's sake while he was still on earth. It has come. There are those who do not accept him or his doctrine.

"Just today," continued Philip, "we heard news of the first martyr for the cause of Christ. Sad to say but he was one of the Seven whom I am numbered with. He was like a younger brother to me. He is to be no more, but he has gone on to be with the Lord. My heart is filled with pain tonight as I tell you these things."

"Who is it, Father?" Charitine asked breathlessly.

"You must be proud of him for he died a noble death. It was Stephen, our very own Stephen, so young and full of faith!" answered Philip.

Charitine moaned softly and slumped to the floor making low groaning sounds as if the pain of the news was too unbearable.

"Children," Philip reminded them, "remember when your mother died, we called on the Comforter to come? We must again pray and ask him to come."

Together they knelt on the plaster floor and prayed to God and asked for his divine comfort to come. Once again they felt a presence enter the room and comfort them as they were praying.

Charitine looked up with tears still wet on her cheeks and said, "Father, I will teach this gospel. I will take his place. I cannot do what he did, but I will do everything I can do for the cause of Christ on earth."

"Oh, Charitine, I'm so proud of you," Philip said as he clumsily held her close trying to take the place of a mother.

To all the girls he said, "We will be strong. We will do all we can no matter what happens! We will not compromise, but we will give ourselves as a family to the greatest cause on earth. Now, let us prepare for bed, get a good night's rest and let the future rest in God's hands."

So thus the day ended with tenderness and love bonding Philip's family closer together than ever before.

Chapter 6

Entering into Jerusalem on the day of Stephen's funeral, Philip and his daughters were joined by many other believers. There was much wailing and lamenting over him as they carried him to his burial. More disturbing than Stephen's death was a new threat. It was the talk of the town. Though Stephen was eliminated, the dangers to the new Christian faith did not go away.

The young man named Saul who had watched Stephen be stoned to death was now in Jerusalem. He was there for one purpose: to persecute the Christians. He was going into their homes, arresting them, treating them roughly and casting them into prison. He was crazy with malicious zeal against the new Church. He did not spare men or women—everyone who believed in Jesus was treated with scorn and disdain.

Approaching the temple, Philip's family saw John who welcomed them warmly. Philip asked him who the young Saul was and where he came from.

"It is reported that he is a Hellenic Jew, from Tarsus in Cilicia," answered John. "He has been trained as a tentmaker but he is also very intense about his Jewish faith. Seems to be fanatical about it."

"What is to become of all of us?" asked Philip. "Several of our friends are in prison right now simply because they believe Jesus was the Christ."

John answered in thoughtful tones, "We will continue to believe and preach what Jesus told us and what we have experienced no matter what comes!"

Philip said, "Ah! yes, that is my conviction, John."

As Philip's family was talking with John, other believers came and greeted them. As they talked they discovered that many of them were moving into other Judean cities and Samaria, except the Apostles.

On the way home later that day Philip seemed deep in thought when finally Hermoine questioned him, "Father, why are you so quiet?"

"Girls, I am feeling strong that the Spirit wants me to go and preach in Samaria," Philip told them.

With shock Irais exclaimed, "You, Father?"

"Yes, Irais, me. I know I have not preached a lot, but this is burning deep within me and those people need the gospel of Jesus Christ," Philip replied with intensity.

"But they are not Jews," Eutychiane said with a question in her voice.

"Peter preached that this experience was for everyone, and if it were not for them why would Jesus have spent time with the woman at the well when he was on earth? I believe he paved the way for the gospel to be brought to the Samaritans," Philip answered.

"But Father, what will your Jewish friends think?" asked Irais.

"Right now with all the persecution going on, no one is going to be very concerned about who hears the gospel. Many are just trying to stay alive," said Philip.

They finally reached their home and when they entered inside Philip called them all around him. He said, "Girls, I will be leaving early in the morning to go to Samaria. You keep things in order while I am gone. Do not go into the City, but stay in much prayer for me and also for those being persecuted. Take this time to prepare yourself to be able to teach later on. I will be back, so have courage for the days ahead. There is food for you to eat while I am gone: vegetables in the garden, dried fruits, nuts and grains. I pray God will overshadow you and keep you and cause his face to shine upon you while I am gone."

"Oh, Father, don't go!" exclaimed Charitine.

"The Spirit has bade me go. I must go, but it will not be for long. I shall return soon," Philip reassured her.

Good nights were said and all lay quiet under the stars, but there was a great stirring taking place that would soon involve the Roman government.

The next day Philip began his journey to Samaria. As he walked he prayed for what was ahead. All of Philip's fears vanished when he entered the city and started preaching. Everyone he preached to received his word with joy. Not only did he preach but he started casting unclean spirits out of people and healing those that were lame.

Joy Haney

Many miracles were accomplished at the hand of Philip by the name of Jesus and everyone that believed was baptized in the name of Jesus.

As the gospel began to take hold of the people it caught the attention of a man called Simon, who was a sorcerer. He had bewitched many of them so that they looked upon him as a great man, and many said of him, "This man is the great power of God." They held him in high esteem for he had used sorcery on them. When Simon saw the great miracles Philip was performing he said, "I believe. I want to be baptized also."

Meanwhile, the Apostles at Jerusalem heard about the great revival in Samaria and that even the sorcerer was baptized, so they sent Peter and John down to help Philip. When they arrived they found out that the people had been baptized in the name of Jesus, but they had not received the Holy Ghost. So Peter and John laid hands on them and they received the Holy Ghost.

When Simon saw the power in the laying on of hands he offered to buy it. Peter looked at him and said, "You cannot buy this power. Repent and ask God to forgive you for trying to equate money with God's power."

As the people saw that Simon had limited power, but that God had all power, great revival flourished not only in Samaria but in many surrounding Samaritan villages.

Early the next morning a visible presence from another world entered the room where Philip was praying. He looked and saw that it was an angel. He gazed reverently upon the angel as the angel spoke, "Philip, arise, and go toward the south unto the way that goes down from Jerusalem unto Gaza, the desert."

When the angel disappeared from out of the room, Philip, struck with awe, arose and made plans to leave immediately for Gaza, which was one of the five chief cities of Philistine, a distance of two miles from the shore of the Mediterranean, and on the high road from Egypt to Joppa.

Philip walked until he reached the desert area and, strangely, there was a man sitting in a chariot that seemed to be waiting for him.

The Spirit spoke to Philip and said, "Go near, and join yourself to this chariot."

Philip ran to the chariot and he heard the man reading aloud. Philip recognized that the reading was from the writings of the prophet Isaiah so he said, "Do you understand what you are reading?"

The man in the chariot said, "How can I, except some man should guide me. Do you understand this?"

"Yes," Philip answered, "and not only do I understand it but the Spirit sent me to you."

"Come up and sit with me in the chariot and let us discuss it," said the man. "I am from Ethiopia, a eunuch of great authority under Candace, queen of the Ethiopians. I am in charge of all her treasures, and am on my way home from Jerusalem where I have been to worship."

Philip said, "I heard you reading about he who was led as a sheep to the slaughter; and like a lamb dumb before his shearer, so opened he not his mouth."

The man said, "I pray you, of whom is the prophet speaking? Of himself, or of some other man?"

With joy Philip answered him, "The prophet was talking about Jesus. Jesus came to earth to save his people from their sins, but was rejected by many of them. They crucified him, buried him and he rose again and has ascended into heaven. But he has commanded all men to repent of their sins, and to be baptized in his name and then they would receive the

Holy Ghost with the evidence of speaking in other tongues."

As they talked they were traveling slowly until they came to a body of water and the man said, "See, here is water; what does hinder me to be baptized?"

Philip said, "If you believe with all your heart, you may."

The man replied with fervency, "I believe that Jesus Christ is the Son of God."

Then he commanded the chariot to be still, while he and Philip climbed down and entered into the water. Philip immersed the man under water in the name of Jesus and when the man came up out of the water the most phenomenal thing took place: The Spirit of the Lord caught Philip up and transported him to Azotus.

The eunuch shook his head in amazement, "I've never seen anything like this before. One minute here, the next minute gone. I have never felt so clean and I have never heard anything so powerful before."

So it was that he went on his way rejoicing, thinking of the miraculous last few hours.

Philip preached in Azotus, then went to Joppa where he preached Jesus. There were many converts that received the Spirit and were baptized. Among them was a woman named Dorcas, who was a skilled seamstress. He then went to the city of Caesarea and preached to them also.

After this whirlwind of preaching and evangelizing Philip felt a need to go home, which he did. When he arrived home, his daughters flung themselves into his arms saying, "Oh, Father, we missed you so much. Wait until you hear all that has been happening while you have been gone."

"Well," Philip said laughingly, "Let us go in and eat first. I have missed your delicious cooking while I have been away."

The girls could not do enough. They drew warm water, washed his feet, got him something to drink and fussed over him while dinner was being prepared.

After dinner they climbed the narrow stairs to the flat roof to enjoy the evening breeze. As they seated themselves Philip said, "Tell me all about it. You seem to be bursting with news."

Hermoine began, "I know you told us to stay close to home, but one of the neighbors fell sick and as I was out of a certain medicine, I had to go into the City to purchase some. While there the City was buzzing with the most unbelievable news since the Feast of Weeks outpouring of the Spirit."

Irais chimed in, "You know that young Pharisee named Saul that was threatening all the Christians? Well, he had received special orders from the high priest to go to Damascus and find the Christian men and women there and bring them bound to prison."

Charitine interrupted, "Oh, let me tell! While he was walking along there came a great light from heaven and shone all around him. It was so bright it blinded him and he fell down to the ground shaking. Out of the heavens a voice spoke which said, 'Saul, Saul, why are you persecuting me?'"

Eutychiane added, "The men that were with him were trembling because they could hear a voice but could not see anyone at all. As he lay shaking on the ground the voice answered him saying, 'I am Jesus whom you persecute: it is hard for you to kick against the pricks.'"

Irais breathlessly continued, "Saul, being filled with awe asked, 'What would you have me to do?' And the Lord answered and told him to go to the city of Damascus and he would receive instructions what to do. But when Saul got up off the ground, he was blind, so the men that were with him led him

Joy Haney

into the city. He stayed there three days without seeing, eating, or drinking."

"The rest of the story," said Hermoine, "is that the Lord visited a disciple in Damascus named Ananias in a vision and told him to go to a street called Straight. He was to go to the house of Judas and ask for a man named Saul of Tarsus because he was praying. Then while Saul was praying he saw a vision also of a man named Ananias putting his hand on him, causing him to receive his sight."

Eutychiane added, "Ananias did what I would have done. He told the Lord that Saul had done much evil in Jerusalem to the saints and that he had gained authority to harm the saints in Damascus. But the Lord told him that Saul was a chosen vessel to bear the name of Jesus before the Gentiles, and kings, and the children of Israel."

Philip shook his head in disbelief, saying, "This is incredible, but I believe it because of all that has happened since Pentecost."

Irais said, "Father, when Ananias went to Saul it happened just like the Lord said. Saul received his sight. Not only that, but he also received the Spirit and was baptized. The thing that is causing quite a stir is that he went straight to the synagogues and started preaching about Jesus and now the people are confused. They even tried to kill him, but the disciples in Damascus helped him escape by letting him down over the wall in a basket at night."

"The troubling thing is," added Hermoine, "when I was in the City there was dissension among the brethren what to do. Most of them were afraid of him, but kind-hearted Barnabas took him in and gave him hospitality. He has been with him all the time since trying to help him make the transition from persecutor to preacher. Quite a change, isn't it?"

"My, my it is all so astonishing," said Philip. "The rapid events that have taken place since the ascension of Jesus."

"Oh, Father, something else," said Eutychiane, "Peter went to Joppa. Remember the place you wrote us about where you preached? Well, when he got there the disciples were in mourning because Dorcas had died."

"Oh, yes, I remember her as one of the converts," said Philip.

"Well," continued Eutychiane, "When Peter arrived in Joppa, the people heard about it and they sent for Peter to come and pray for the dead body. When he got there, the widows were weeping and showing him all the garments Dorcas had made for them. Then Peter did a strange thing. He told them all to leave the room and then he just knelt down and prayed. Then he spoke to her and told her to rise and the most incredible thing happened. She opened her eyes and when she saw Peter, she sat up. Peter then called all the mourners in and they were in shock and many more people believed in Jesus Christ after the miracle of raising the dead took place."

Philip said, "Girls, we need to praise God for these great and notable things that have taken place. Surely the glory of the Lord is not only in us but it is around us. This is a new day for those that believe in Jesus and his power."

There on the flat roof of their home, they gave praise and thanksgiving for the wonderful things that were taking place among the new believers. Then Philip shared with them the things that had happened to him.

He said, "While I was gone an angel visited me also and the Spirit transported me through the air from Gaza to Azotus. It was unbelievable, but it really happened."

"Father," the girls screamed in unison, "Why didn't you tell us sooner?"

Philip chuckled, "You were all so talkative about all that has been happening that all I could do was listen. I knew my news would wait."

"Tell us all about it," they all chimed in.

And so the evening ended with the four daughters listening in rapt attention to the extraordinary events that had transpired in the life of Philip, their father.

Chapter 7

The next day brought more news about the rapid pace of the growth of the new church throughout the land. When Philip went into the city to share with James all that had happened in the past few months, he received an earful also.

While sitting around the table breaking bread and fellowshipping with James and several of the disciples there was discussion of Peter's stay in Joppa.

"Did you know he is living with Simon the tanner there?" asked Nicanor.

"No, I had not heard that," answered Philip.

"Something else," Nicanor continued. "Peter was on the housetop in prayer at noon and he became very hungry. While his host made the food ready Peter fell into a trance. He saw the heaven open and a sheet was let down full of wild beasts, fowls and creeping things in the earth."

Timon interrupted, "Yes, then there came a voice telling him to rise and eat. And Peter said, 'No, Lord, I have never eaten anything common or unclean.' Then the voice spoke again and said, 'What God has cleansed call not common.' This happened three times and while Peter doubted and pondered about it, a messenger went up to Peter and told him there were some men standing at the gate asking for him; they were sent from a man named Cornelius, a centurion of the band called the Italian band."

James said, "Now remember, Peter was still thinking about the vision while this was taking place on the ground below. Suddenly the Spirit spoke to him and told him to go down and not to doubt, for three men were seeking him and the Lord had sent them. So Peter went down and said, 'I'm the man you are looking for. What do you want?'"

Parmenas added, "The men sent from Cornelius told him that an angel had told Cornelius to come to this house and get Peter to preach to his household. So Peter left Joppa and went to Caesarea and preached Jesus to the household of Cornelius, and while Peter was preaching the Holy Ghost fell on them. Peter and the others with him heard them speak with tongues and magnify God. They were astonished that Gentiles could receive the Holy Ghost.

"Then Peter commanded all of them to be baptized in the name of Jesus and they all were immersed in the water according to the instructions of Jesus."

Philip shook his head in amazement. "What next?" Then rising he looked around at the group of men and said, "The fellowship has been wonderful, but I must go now. May God be with all of you until we meet again."

And so Philip started on the journey towards home.

37-41 A.D.

Relations between Rome and the Jews became more hostile with the new reign of Gaius, or Caligula, the Caesar. He was tall with a pallid complexion, hairy body, and was badly built and bald. He became obsessed with the idea that he was a living god and he demanded that his subjects acknowledge his divinity.

A group of Gentiles in Jamnia erected an altar to him. The local Jews were enraged and immediately toppled the altar. When the incident was reported to Caligula he commanded that a colossal golden statue of himself be erected at the temple in Jerusalem.

Anticipating the Jews' hostile reaction, Caligula ordered Petronius, the Roman governor of Syria, to lead an army into Judea. If any refused to admit the soldiers Caligula ordered, they were to be killed and the whole nation enslaved. When Petronius arrived in Ptolemais, there came tens of thousands of the Jews to offer their petitions to him, that he would not compel them to transgress and violate the law of their forefathers.

They cried, "If you are resolved to erect the statue, you must first kill us, for while we are alive we cannot permit such things."

Petronius grew angry and shouted at them, "If indeed I were myself Emperor, and were at liberty to follow my own inclination, your words would be justly spoken to me; but now Caesar has sent me. I am under the necessity of being sub-servient to his decrees. If I disobey it will bring destruction."

Then the Jews cried back, "Since, therefore, you are so disposed, O Petronius! that you will not disobey Caligula's epistles, neither will we transgress the commands of our law."

When Petronius saw by their words that they were determined, he went to Tiberius also. He found the same thing there. Tens of thousands stood against erecting the new statue in the temple. Petronius said to them, "Will you then make war with Caesar, without considering his great preparations for war, and your own weakness?"

They replied, "We will not by any means make war with him; but still we will die before we will see our laws transgressed."

Then they threw themselves down upon their faces, and stretched out their throats and said they were ready to be slain. They did this for forty days together, and in the meantime left off the tilling of their ground. Thus they continued firm in their resolution, and proposed to themselves to die willingly, rather than to see the dedication of the statue.

Petronius sent word back to Caligula and interceded for the Jews, which made Caligula very angry, but King Agrippa influenced Caligula to back off and give it time. Caligula then sent word to Petronius to hold off, but then a few days later retracted his statement and sent another letter to Petronius.

In the meantime, Caligula did not only demonstrate his madness to the Jews but also to tens of thousands of the Romans. He asserted his own divinity and insisted on greater honors to be paid him by his subjects than are due to mankind. He also visited the temple of Jupiter and boldly stated that he was the brother of Jupiter. Such atrocities could be borne no longer by the Romans. Several plots to assassinate Caligula began to form. One such plot was started by Cherea. Caligula had set him to require and collect dues and tributes and also made him torture people that did not please Caligula. Cherea shared his anguish with Clement, general of the army, and Papinius, a tribune.

Cherea cried passionately, "We may indeed pretend in words, that Caligula is the person unto whom the cause of such miseries ought to be imputed; but, in the opinion of such as are able to judge uprightly, it is I, O Clement! and this Papinius, and before us thou thyself, who bring these tortures upon the Romans, and upon all mankind. It is not done by our being sub-servient to the commands of Caligula, but it is done by our own consent; for whereas it is in our power to put an end to the life of this man, who hath so terribly injured the citizens and his subjects. We are his guard in mischief and his executioners, instead of his soldiers, and are the instruments of his cruelty. We bear weapons, not for our liberty, not for the Roman government, but only for his preservation, who hath enslaved both their bodies and their minds; and we are everyday polluted with the blood that we shed, and the torments we afflict upon others."

Cherea struck a responsive chord not only in his two friends but in other senators. The plot was well-planned and the fateful day arrived at the time of the sacrifice to Augustus Caesar. After the sacrifice Caligula went into the theater to watch the shows. He then left early to go down to the baths and when he entered a narrow passage there he was slain. His reign ended in blood just as it had been lived.

Although his death stopped the erection of the statue in the temple at Jerusalem, persecution against the Church was escalating as each day passed. The services that were held together by the new believers were considered sacred, and as the blood of the martyrs flowed, the miracles increased as did the growth of the Church.

Chapter 8

44 A.D.

Along with the fervor of the growth of the early Church, an ill wind began to blow against the praying, faithful Christians, and sharp persecution was raised against them. They were starting to feel the scourge of the Roman whip in cities across the land. Timon and Parmenas, two of the seven deacons, were martyred; one in Phillippi, the other in Macedonia.

Shortly before the death of King Herod Agrippa, in the spring of 44, he made an attack on the Church, and determined to make a truly lasting effect by striking at their leaders. He chose James, the leader in Jerusalem, and had him beheaded. This pleased the religious Jews: the high priests and their followers. The growth of the Church had stirred up the envy of the Jews, and the enthusiasm with which they welcomed the execution of James, the brother of John, encouraged the King to throw Peter into prison. He delivered him to four quaternions of soldiers to keep him until Easter when he would bring him forth to the people to decide his fate.

Word was circulated house to house among the Christians in the City and surrounding areas to pray without ceasing, and so prayer meetings were set up in different houses. While the Christians were praying one night something spectacular happened. Peter, who was asleep between two soldiers and was bound with two chains with keepers standing by the door, was suddenly awakened. An angel appeared from heaven which shone a bright light, smote Peter on the side, raised him up and told him to get up quickly. When he stood up his chains fell off. The angel told him to gird himself and to put his shoes on; so he did. Then the angel started walking and told Peter to follow him.

They walked through both the first ward and the second ward until they came to an iron gate that led into the city. When they got there the door opened all by itself. Peter thought it was a vision until

Joy Haney

finally he came to himself. He felt the night air, saw that the angel was gone and began walking briskly to the house of Mary, the mother of John Mark, where many people were gathered praying.

When the wicked, diabolical King found out about the disappearance of Peter he had the keepers of the prison put to death. Not long after this, Herod went to Caesarea and gave a speech at the palace there. The people that heard him said it was the voice of a god, not a man, and immediately the Lord God smote him because he did not give God the glory. He then was eaten of worms and died shortly thereafter.

After the death of King Herod and the increase of persecution at Jerusalem, Philip took up permanent residence in Caesarea[1] where he and his

---

[1] Caesarea was a sea coast on the Mediterranean known for its great harbor. Vast stones were sunk in the sea to the depth of twenty fathoms, forming a stupendous breakwater, curving round so as to afford complete protection from the southwesterly winds, and open only on the north. Caesarea was closely associated with Rome and its Emperors, and its population contained many heathen strangers. Because of the famous port, the foreign influence was great.

Near the shore was a large theater where Roman shows were shown often. Also, approaching the city from the sea, one could see a temple dedicated to Caesar and to Rome, which contained colossal statues. (continued...)

daughters taught the people the ways of the Lord and strengthened the disciples there.

49 A.D.

Claudius, the Emperor of Rome, issued an edict for the banishment of all the Jews from Rome. The identification of the Christians with the Jews was not the result of a mistake. They were Jews, and the Christians who had been sojourners from Rome in Jerusalem on the day of Pentecost and had received the infilling of the Holy Ghost were regarded simply as a sect, but one which bothered the Roman Emperor. They were followers of Christ and were literally spreading this new doctrine everywhere— even in Caesar's household. (Among those banished were Aquila and Priscilla, who went to Corinth, where they came into contact with Paul.)

54 A.D.

Persecution was still strong against the Church and increasing rapidly. Philip, one of the twelve,

---

Two aqueducts from Carmel brought the waters of the Zerka, or Crocodile River, to the city. The Romans built them with round arches, running over the swamps, and a tunnel through the cliffs, with rock-cut staircases descending in wells.

was scourged, thrown into prison, and afterwards crucified.

In Rome, Nero became the new Emperor on the throne. Born in A.D. 37, Nero and his parents, Domitius and Agrippina, all belonged to the Family of the Caesars. Nero was destined from childhood for the imperial throne by his ambitious mother, who in A.D. 49 secured her own marriage to the Emperor Claudius, her uncle; then the betrothal of Nero and Octavia, the daughter of Claudius and Messalina (his former wife). In A.D. 50, Nero was adopted as the Emperor's son and designated successor, superseding Claudius' own son, Britannicus. When Claudius died suddenly in A.D. 54, Nero, mainly through his mother's strategy, was peacefully accepted as Emperor by the army, senate, and people.

In the first year of his reign, at the age of 25, he had a trusted servant poison his brother, Britannicus, because he did not want any imperial rivals. Nero told everyone that his brother had died in a fit of epilepsy.

Nero also orchestrated the death of Agrippina, his own mother, the reason being that Nero's mistress, Poppaea (wife of Otho who afterwards became Emperor) desired to be his wife but

Agrippina's influence stood in the way. From A.D. 58, Nero's connection with Poppaea and her fatal influence over him became the chief factor in his thorough demoralization, and a direct or indirect occasion of many of his crimes. Poppaea coveted the position of Empress, and determined to secure the divorce and removal of the neglected Octavia, Nero's wife.

Nero and Poppaea schemed and diabolically worked against Octavia. Witnesses were brought forth who told lies about Octavia and she was pronounced guilty of infidelity, was divorced and later murdered. Poppaea was married to Nero shortly afterward and became Empress.

57 A.D.

During this time Philip's household was very blessed with the arrival of the Apostle Paul and his companions. All the bustle, excitement and heartfelt welcome made Paul feel like royalty. The hospitality was so great that he made his abode at Philip's home for many days where they had wonderful fellowship and sharing of the Word. The saints in Caesarea were blessed to have Paul minister at their services and many great things took place.

One mid-morning a prophet, Agabus, who lived near Caesarea, arrived at Philip's house where he was welcomed joyously. He was not so joyous though, because he had words of prophecy that would bring sorrow to Paul. Agabus took the girdle of Paul and fastened it around his own hands and feet and said, "Thus says the Holy Ghost: so shall the Jews at Jerusalem bind the man to whom this girdle belongs, and they shall deliver him into the hands of the Gentiles."

After hearing this prophecy, Philip's daughters, as well as some of Paul's friends—Luke, Aristarchus, and Trophimus—wept and implored him not to go to Jerusalem. Paul spoke with resolution and purpose as he responded to their pleas. He said, "I am ready not only to be bound, but to die at Jerusalem for the name of the Lord Jesus."

Because no one could change Paul's mind, the carriages were brought forth and made ready for the journey. Philip's family and several of the disciples in Caesarea went with Paul, as well as an old disciple, Mnason of Cyprus. When they arrived in Jerusalem, they were received with joy with the symbol of brotherhood, the kiss of peace, which was exchanged between the Christians on every occasion of public as well as private meeting.

After being in some of the meetings and talking with some of the Christians there, Philip and Luke talked together about some of the changes that seemed to be taking place. Luke said, "The atmosphere among some of the believers has changed somewhat since the outpouring of the Holy Ghost 28 years ago. Although there appeared to be a show of harmony at Paul's meeting today, underneath lurked an element of discord, which threatened to disturb it."

Philip responded, "Some of the Christians shared with me their concern about what is taking place, also. They said that the Church here in Jerusalem has developed a small Pharisaic faction that continually strives to turn Christianity into a sect of Judaism. In fact, this group has recently sent emissaries into the Gentile churches and endeavored to alienate the minds of Paul's converts away from him and his teachings. These men are restless agitators."

"Yes," replied Luke, "some of the Christians left in Jerusalem after the scattering during the severe persecution fourteen years ago are yet weak, and have not attained to the fullness of the Christian faith. Their minds are still in a state of transition between the Law and the Gospel of Jesus, the Christ.

"At Paul's meeting today with the elders, they shared with him the unrest and dislike some of the Jews had toward him. They suggested to him strongly that he needed to go into the temple with four men who had taken a Nazarite vow and purify himself with them," finished Luke.

The next day, which was the great feast of Pentecost, Paul proceeded with the four Christian Nazarites to the temple. It was customary among the Jews for those who had received deliverance from any great peril, or who for other causes desired publicly to testify of their dedication to God, to take upon themselves the vow of the Nazarite. This vow was normally for a thirty-day period. During this time the Nazarite was not to drink strong drink or cut his hair. At the end of thirty days he went to the temple with certain offerings and his hair was cut off and burned upon the altar.

When Paul entered the temple, he announced to the priest that the period of the Nazarite vow which his friends had taken was accomplished, and he waited within the sacred enclosure till the necessary offerings were made for each of them, and their hair cut off and burnt in the sacred fire.

The plan probably would have worked to conciliate the Jews that resided in Jerusalem, but the celebration of the festival attracted multitudes and the temple was thronged with worshippers from every land. Among them were some of the Asiatic Jews who had been defeated by Paul's arguments in the synagogue of Ephesus. Since they had never found opportunity for revenge in their own city, they now found a good reason to stir up trouble. They cried out loudly, "Men of Israel, help! This is the man that teaches all men everywhere against the people, the law, and this place. This man has also profaned the Holy Place by introducing Greeks into it."[2]

---

[2] The Outer Court of the Temple was shaped in a square; a strong wall enclosed it; the sides corresponded to the four quarters of the heavens, and each was a stadium or a furlong in length. Its pavement of stone was of various colors: and it was surrounded by a covered colonnade, the roof of which was of costly cedar, and was supported on lofty and massive columns of the Corinthian order, and of the whitest marble. On three sides there were two rows of columns, but on the southern side the cloister deepened into a fourfold colonnade, the innermost supports of the roof being pilasters in the enclosing wall. About the southeastern angle, where the valley was most depressed below the plateau of the Temple,

The multitude became a mob and they rushed upon Paul, seized him, dragged him out of the temple and tried to kill him. About that time the Roman chief, Claudius Lysias, received word of the uproar. Lysias himself rushed down instantly with a group of Imperial soldiers into the Temple. At the sight of the flashing arms and disciplined movements of the soldiers, and because of their hatred and fear of the Roman authority, the Jewish mob stopped their murderous violence.

Lysias and his soldiers then went directly to Paul and ordered him to be chained by each hand to a soldier, for he suspected that Paul might be the Egyptian rebel that had murdered 400 men and was

---

we are to look for that "Porch of Solomon," and under the colonnades, or on the open arena in the midst. Free access was afforded into this wide enclosure by gates on each of the four sides, one of which on the east was the Royal Gate, and was perhaps identical with the Beautiful Gate, while another on the west was connected with the crowded streets of Mount Zion by a bridge over the intervening valley.

Nearer to the northwestern corner than the center of the square, arose that series of enclosed terraces on the summit of which was the sanctuary. These more sacred limits were fenced off by a low balustrade of stone, with columns at intervals, on which inscriptions in Greek and Latin warned all Gentiles against advancing beyond them on pain of death. It was within this boundary that Paul was accused of having brought his heathen companions.

still on the loose. The rebel had come to Jerusalem and said he was a prophet and influenced a multitude of the common people to go along with him to the Mount of Olives. He had told them that he would show them how, at his spoken command, the walls of Jerusalem would fall down, and he promised to procure them an entrance into the city through those walls when they were fallen down. When Felix ordered his soldiers to go after the Egyptian, he had escaped.

So thinking Paul was that Egyptian, he asked the multitude who Paul was, and everyone started screaming and hollering so many different answers to his question that he ordered the soldiers to take Paul to the barracks in the Castle. The crowd grew so threatening that the soldiers had to carry Paul while the mob cried, "Away with him. Away with him!"

When they entered the fortress, Paul turned to the commanding officer and spoke to him in Greek, "May I speak with you?" It startled Claudius Lysias when he heard his prisoner speak Greek, and so he told Paul that maybe he was mistaken in supposing him to be the Egyptian ringleader of the late rebellion.

Joy Haney

Paul told him he was not an Egyptian, but a Jew, then he asked if he could talk to the people. Surprisingly Lysias granted his request.

While Paul stood on the stairs he addressed the people and told about where he came from, his experience on the Damascus Road, his conversion, and Stephen's death. They listened and were half-way convinced until he mentioned his ministry to the Gentiles. Their pride bore down every argument which could influence their reason. They could not bear the thought of uncircumcised heathens being made equal to the sons of Abraham. They grew so angry that they again shouted vehemently, "Away with such a fellow from the earth. It is not fit that he should live."

The crowd grew so violent that they took off their outer garments and threw dust into the air until Lysias commanded that Paul be taken in for a scourging and questioning. Paul then asked if it was lawful for a Roman that was uncondemned to be scourged. When Lysias heard that Paul was a Roman he became afraid. The magic of the Roman law produced its effect in a minute's time.

In this moment of hesitation, it was settled that Paul would go before the high priests and the Sanhedrin the next day.

Chapter 9

Paul slept in a Roman fortress that night, awaiting his appearance before the Sanhedrin.

The following morning, when Paul entered the Sanhedrin, of which he himself had once been a member, he recognized his old friends and addressed them as such. His unflinching look of conscious integrity and his confident words offended them. The priest became so enraged that he commanded those who stood near Paul to strike him on the mouth. This brutal insult roused the Apostle's feelings and he exclaimed, "God shall smite you, you whited wall: for you sit to judge me after the law, and do you command me to be smitten contrary to the law?"

The other members of the Sanhedrin were shocked by Paul's outburst and cried out, "Do you dare revile God's high priest?"

Paul immediately was contrite and told them he did not know he was the high priest. The end result of this meeting was that the Pharisees and the Sadducees got into a fight and there was such dissension that the chief captain again took him by force from among them and took him into the castle where he spent another night.

During the night the Lord came and stood by Paul and told him that he would go to Rome and witness for him. But the next day more than forty Jews banded together and made a pact with one another that they would not eat nor drink until they had killed Paul.

They went to the chief priests and elders and told them what they had conspired to do. They told them to bring Paul to them as to inquire of him some information and when they did the men promised that they would kill him. The only thing that stopped them was that Paul's nephew heard about it and went straight to the castle and told Paul about it. Paul then called one of the centurions to him and asked him to take his nephew to Claudius Lysias. When Lysias, the chief captain, heard this bit of news, he told the boy not to tell anyone of what he had heard.

In the meantime, Lysias called two trusted officers and told them to get ready 200 of the legionary soldiers, seventy of the cavalry, and 200 spearmen to leave at 9:00 that same night to go to Caesarea unto Felix, the governor.

And so it was the large company of soldiers stole away into the night guarding *one* prisoner. Paul, with not much bodily presence, was shaking a world through the new power of the Holy Ghost that he had experienced in Damascus.

The route they traveled to Caesarea took him away from the conspiracies of the Jews and placed him under the protection of Felix. The road ran northward for about three hours, along the high mountainous region which divides the valley of the Jordan from the great western plain of Judea. About midnight they reached Gophna. After a short halt, they turned towards the coast on the left. As they began to descend on the Roman pavement among the western valleys of the mountain country, they startled the shepherds on the hills of Ephraim and roused the village peasants who woke only to curse their oppressor, as they heard the hoofs of the horses on the pavement and the well-known tramp of the Roman soldiers.

They proceeded, still descending over a rocky tract with little cultivation and thinly sprinkled shrubbery, until about daybreak when they came to the ridge of the last hill that overlooked the plain of Sharon. Following the road they turned northward across the rich land of the plain of Sharon, through fields of wheat and barley which were almost ready for harvest.

On the east were the mountains of Samaria, rising gradually above each other, and bounding the plain in that direction. On the left lay a line of low wooded hills, shutting it in from the sea. Between this higher and lower range, but on the level ground, in a place well-watered and richly wooded, was the town of Antipatris.

At this point, the foot-soldiers returned to Jerusalem, as they were no longer necessary to secure Paul's safety. The rest of the group pressed on with their weary horses until they reached Caesarea in the afternoon. The centurion in command proceeded straight to the magnificent Herod's palace, which was the governor's residence, and where the regular barracks for the garrison were stationed. As they approached Felix, the governor, he handed over his prisoner and presented him the dispatch from Claudius Lysias.

Felix raised his eyes from the paper and asked, "To what province does he belong?"

It was the first question a Roman governor would naturally ask in such a case. Having heard that Paul was a native of the province of Cilicia,[3] Felix simply ordered him to be kept in Herod's praetorium or judgment hall. Then he turned to Paul and said, "I will hear and decide your cause when your accusers are also come."

---

[3] Cilicia was a country in the southeast corner of Asia Minor, on the coast, adjoining Syria. It was commonly divided into two territories, 1) on the west (reaching as far as Pamphylia) Cilicia Tracheia, a land of lofty and rugged mountains, drained by the considerable river Calycadrus, and 2) on the east, Cilicia Pedias, a low-lying and very fertile plain between the sea and the mountain ranges, Raurus and Amanus. The entire double country is summed up as Cilicia in Acts 27:5, a geographical description of the lands touching the Cyprian Sea. But elsewhere it is clear that only the civilized and peaceful Cilicia was subject to Roman rule. Paul lived in the city of Tarsus, the chief city of Cilicia. When Paul was a child, Tarsus stood before the world at the entrance of the greatest province of the East as a metropolis, a free city with a free harbor. It was a large and fertile territory and a center of Roman imperial partisanship. The Tarsian university, which Paul attended, was the finest in the land.

So Paul was bound in chains, but though his body was bound, his soul and spirit were not.

Philip's household was in a state of distress over this latest turn of events. They had just arrived home from Jerusalem a week ago and now one of the disciples had brought the latest news about Paul, who had been a guest in their home for many days.

Paul's arrival to Caesarea in bonds brought many of the disciples together that evening. As they approached Philip's residence, which had been chosen as the meeting place, there seemed to be a feeling of menace in the air. Joining with other believers they began to pray together for the recent happenings that affected all the believers of Christ.

Philip addressed the group with words of destiny. "Fellow Christians, new persecutions have arisen. Our own dear Paul even now is in prison. None of us know how this will affect all of us and many other believers in every city and province. How far it will spread no one knows. Whatever happens, stay true to the doctrines of Christ, retain your zeal, continue to fellowship, and reach new ones with the gospel of Jesus Christ, our Lord. We will not be afraid! We will go forward with the power of the Spirit in our souls, vision in our minds, and love in our hearts! We will continue to evangelize even as dark days are approaching. The light of the gospel must reach into every village and town."

As Philip finished speaking, the believers that were gathered together burst forth in praise to God for choosing them to be filled with his Spirit. They gave their pledge that they would follow him, no matter what the future held.

FIVE DAYS LATER

Pompous Ananias, the High Priest, and several of the elders of the Sanhedrin, along with Tertullus, the orator, arrived to voice their accusations against Paul.

As the trial opened, Tertullus was given the floor on which he first of all praised and honored Felix. Then he brought three accusations against Paul, charging him first with causing factious disturbances among all the Jews throughout the Empire, which was an offense against the Roman government, and amounted to treason against the Emperor. Secondly, he accused him of being the leader of the sect of the Nazarenes, which involved heresy against the law of Moses. Thirdly, he accused Paul of attempting to profane the temple at Jerusalem (an offense not only against the Jewish Law, but also against the Roman, which protected the Jews in the exercise of their worship). He concluded with deviations from the truth that Lysias, the commander of the garrison, had forcibly taken the prisoner away when the Jews were about to judge him by their own ecclesiastical law, and had improperly brought the matter before Felix.

The Jews who were present vehemently assented to this presentation of Tertullus, making no secret of their animosity against Paul. Felix then turned to Paul and beckoned for him to speak.

Paul looked around at his accusers and then directed his comments to the governor, saying, "Knowing, as I do, that you have been judge over the nation for many years, I defend myself in the matters brought against me with greater confidence. For it is in your power to learn, that only twelve days have passed since I went up to Jerusalem to worship. And neither in the temple, nor in the synagogues, nor in the streets, did they find me disputing with any man, or causing any disorderly concourse of people; nor can they prove against me the things whereof they now accuse me.

"But this I acknowledge to you, that I follow the opinion, which they call a sect, and thus worship the

God of my fathers. I believe all things which are written in the law and in the Prophets; and I hold a hope towards God, which my accusers themselves entertain, that there will be a resurrection of the dead, both of the just and the unjust. Wherefore also I myself strive earnestly to keep a conscience always void of offense towards God and man.

"Now after several years I came hither, to bring alms to my nation, and offerings to the Temple. And they found me so doing in the Temple, after I had undergone purification; not gathering a multitude, nor causing a tumult; but certain Jews from Asia discovered me, who ought to have been here before you to accuse me, if they had anything to object against me.

"Or let these my accusers themselves say whether they found me guilty of any offense, when I was brought before the Sanhedrin; except it be for these words only which I cried out as I stood in the midst of them, concerning the resurrection of the dead, I am called in question before you this day."

Paul's words were full of truth and harmonized entirely with the statement contained in the dispatch from Claudius Lysias. Felix was not a stranger to the new Christian religion for he had resided in Caesarea for six years and it had penetrated even among his troops, so he had a more accurate knowledge of their religion than to be easily deceived by the misrepresentation of the Jews.

Even though Felix was a wicked man, he was convinced that Paul was telling the truth, but he could not find it in him to acquit him, so he delayed a judgment saying, "When Lysias, the chief captain shall come down, I will know what to do."

Then he instructed one of the centurions to treat Paul with kindness and consideration, and for him to be able to walk around in a relaxed atmosphere. He also allowed Paul to have his friends come and visit him.

Joy Haney

Chapter 10

Luke and Philip received word from one of the believers that Paul could have visitors. What a stir this created in Philip's household. Hermoine and Charitine immediately set to work preparing a basket of food for Paul, for he was loved by them, having stayed in their home prior to going to Jerusalem, and they knew the foods he preferred.

"Oh, I do hope Paul is released," Hermoine said, looking anxiously at Charitine. "He is such a powerful man in the Spirit!"

"You can be sure, Paul will not waste this opportunity to try to convert others to Christ," responded Charitine. "He is such an intense man! It seems as if he has a fire inside of him at all times."

Pausing and looking thoughtful, she asked, "If they don't release him, what will happen to all the churches?"

Hermoine put another loaf of bread in the basket, adding some dates, figs and honey, talking all the while. "The way things are developing with all the disturbances in the streets, it does not look good for Paul. And with such a coarse and cruel governor, he cannot expect much mercy from him."

"Whatever happens, we will trust in the Lord," Charitine said with feeling, as she snapped the lid shut on the basket prepared for Paul.

Humming to herself she took the basket into the courtyard where her father and Luke were waiting.

"Here it is, Father. Please tell Paul that we are praying for him," she said as she handed him the basket, kissing him lightly on the cheek.

Bidding the two men good day she went and joined her sister in the preparation for the evening meal.

Setting out towards the castle, Philip and Luke passed homes where the smell of fresh bread being baked permeated the air. Waving to friends and talking about recent developments, they soon entered the area where the barracks were located.

With repressed excitement, they went to where the guards were stationed.

Immediately the guard asked them who they had come to see.

"Paul, the Apostle," Luke responded.

"Come this way and you will be able to join Paul for a short visit," the guard told them in clipped tones.

They entered into the area where the prisoners were held and there they were united with Paul. The soldier who was chained together with Paul loosed the band and Paul was able to converse with his two friends in private under the watchful eye of the soldier.

They both embraced Paul and wept upon seeing him again. "May the God of Shalom be with you!" they uttered fervently. "The believers have been praying and fasting for you that God's protection would be with you."

"God has been with me," said Paul. "We have already had two converts added to the faith.[4] Luke,

---

[4] Paul was always chained to a soldier of the guard with his right hand chained to the soldier's left hand. The soldiers, of course, relieved one another in this duty, and thus through the change of guards, Paul's message spread throughout the whole body of soldiers.

they need to be baptized. Will you baptize them for me?"

"As soon as we can make arrangements, we will notify the other believers and have a baptismal service, for there are others that are waiting to be baptized," answered Luke.

"How are all the believers doing during these difficult times?" asked Paul. "Are they still fervent, holding services in their homes and praying for one another?"

"Oh yes! The number of believers is increasing daily. There are many miracles among them. It is causing quite a stir."

"You must go now," the guard interrupted their conversation.

As Philip handed Paul the basket filled with good things, he said, "Here is a basket of food Hermoine and Charitine prepared for you, Paul. They said to tell you they were praying for you."

"Give all the girls my love, Philip. I'll never forget your family's hospitality to me. Greet all the believers for me. Tell them to keep the faith. Be strong in doctrine and fervent in love," Paul admonished them as they said their good-byes.

Several days later, Felix came with his wife, Drusilla, who was a Jewess, and sent for Paul. Drusilla was a granddaughter of Herod the Great, and the youngest daughter of Herod Agrippa I. She first married King Aziz of Emesa on his becoming a Jew, and was unfaithful to him, eventually leaving him. She illegitimately married the Roman governor, Felix, who, enamored of her Oriental beauty, abducted her through the subtlety of Simon, the Jewish sorcerer.

Drusilla was a beautiful but shameless woman. She was about twenty years old at the time of Paul's testimony. Both Drusilla and Felix heard a message they did not expect. As Paul reasoned of righteousness, temperance, and judgment to come, Felix trembled and became afraid. So greatly was Felix moved and disturbed that he dismissed Paul, saying that at a convenient season he would hear him again.

Meanwhile, as Paul was left bound in the prison at Caesarea, and visited often by Philip, Luke, and many other of the believers in Christ, there was a new wave of persecution against the Christians in Rome and elsewhere. The Christians in Caesarea and other cities were beginning to feel the whip of

Rome and wondered how this would affect the Apostle Paul.

Chapter 11

Two years after Felix had placed Paul in bonds, there came a new governor to Caesarea. Festus had been in office only three days when he went up to Jerusalem. As soon as he arrived there, the high priests asked him if he would bring Paul to Jerusalem for a new trial, for they planned to kill him on the way.

Meanwhile in Caesarea some of the Christians had gathered at Philip's house for a special prayer meeting. Charitine, Hermoine, Irais, and Eutychiane all ministered to the needs of the people that came—encouraging them to be strong and to continue in the faith in spite of what was happening in the government and the political world.

After they had prayed the place was shaken with the power of God. Great boldness filled their hearts and they begin to speak with other tongues as they experienced the visitation of the Holy Ghost once more.

Philip stood and encouraged them all to give themselves to the things of God and to continue in the teachings of Jesus Christ the Lord, then asked Luke to address them. Luke stood and shared with them the awful news concerning Matthew.

"My dear brothers and sisters, the days are perilous and many disturbing things are taking place, but we must remember that Jesus said persecutions would come. First of all, we lost Stephen to martyrdom, then James, Timon, Parmenas and others. Now we have received word that Matthew has been thrust through with a spear in the city of Nadabah, Ethiopia. We must be brave and not become afraid. Remember what Paul told us, 'To die is gain!' Be strong in the Lord and in the power of his might in these days that are upon us, for persecution could possibly increase. Recently there has been much rumblings about Nero's cruelty to the Christians. Yes, it will probably increase, but be of good courage, for the Lord will be with you!"

As they fellowshipped one with another they felt new hope rising within them for the days ahead.

While the Church was praying, Festus was still in Jerusalem dealing with the Jews. He told them that Paul would be kept at Caesarea, that he would not be brought to Jerusalem. Then he asked them if they wanted to come down with him and bring accusations against Paul.

Ten days later, Festus went back home to Caesarea. On the following day he called Paul into the judgment hall. When Paul entered he looked around and saw the Jews that were there from Jerusalem.

Festus, being a new leader, wanted to gain favor of those over whom he ruled, so he asked Paul, "Would you rather go up to Jerusalem to be judged there?"

Paul said, "I have not done any wrong to the Jews, as you well know. I stand at Caesar's judgment seat and appeal to Caesar himself."

Festus was surprised by this turn of events, for he knew that as a Roman citizen, Paul had the right to remove his cause from the local jurisdiction and transfer it to the supreme tribunal of the Emperor at Rome.

Paul was taken back to the barracks to await further orders and while waiting continued to write letters to the churches and convert the soldiers.

Caesarea was in a state of excitement. King Agrippa and Bernice had just arrived in town to visit Festus, the governor. After they had been there several days, Festus brought up the subject of Paul's imprisonment and told him of Paul's unusual request. King Agrippa said, "I would also like to hear the man myself."

"Tomorrow, you shall hear him," Festus agreed.

Bernice was the eldest daughter of Herod Agrippa I who ruled from A.D. 38-45, and is described as the one who vexed the Church early on. She was first married to Marcus. After a while she married her uncle, Herod, King of Chaleis. When he died, she was suspected of evil relations with her own brother, Agrippa, in whose company she always appeared.

Paul was brought forth the next day before the assemblage of shameless Bernice, Herod, Festus, the chief captains, and principal men of the city. They in their pomp and glory witnessed his humility and power.

Joy Haney

Festus opened the hearing by telling Agrippa publicly about Paul. Then Agrippa turned to Paul and said condescendingly, "You may speak for yourself."

Paul began to speak and as he spoke his audience trembled. He said, "I think myself happy, King Agrippa, because I shall answer for myself this day before you touching all the things whereof I am accused of the Jews: Especially because I know you to be expert in all customs and questions which are among the Jews: wherefore I beseech thee to hear me patiently.

"My manner of life from my youth, which was at the first among my own nation at Jerusalem, know all the Jews; which knew me from the beginning, if they would testify, that after the most straightest sect of our religion I lived a Pharisee. And now I stand and am judged for the hope of the promise made of God unto our fathers: unto which promise our twelve tribes, instantly serving God day and night, hope to come. For which hope's sake, King Agrippa, I am accused of the Jews.

"Why should it be thought a thing incredible with you, that God should raise the dead? I verily thought with myself, that I ought to do many things contrary to the name of Jesus of Nazareth. Which thing I also did in Jerusalem: and many of the saints did I shut up in prison, having received authority from the chief priests; and when they were put to death, I gave my voice against them. And I punished them often in every synagogue, and compelled them to blaspheme; and being exceedingly mad against them, I persecuted them even unto strange cities.

"Whereupon as I went to Damascus with authority and commission from the chief priests, at midday, O King, I saw in the way a light from heaven, above the brightness of the sun, shining round about me and them which journeyed with me. And when we were all fallen to the earth, I heard a voice speaking unto me, and saying in the Hebrew tongue, 'Saul, Saul, why do you persecute me? It is hard for thee to kick against the pricks.'

"And I said, 'Who are you, Lord?' And he said, 'I am Jesus whom you persecute. But rise, and stand upon your feet: for I have appeared unto you for this purpose, to make you a minister and a witness both of these things which you have seen, and of those things in the which I will appear unto you: delivering you from the people, and from the Gentiles, unto whom now I send you, to open their eyes, and to turn them from darkness to light, and from the power of Satan unto God, that they may receive forgiveness of sins, and inheritance among them which are sanctified by faith that is in me.'

"Whereupon, O King Agrippa, I was not disobedient unto the heavenly vision: but showed first unto them of Damascus, and at Jerusalem, and throughout all the coasts of Judea, and then to the Gentiles, that they should repent and turn to God, and do works meet for repentance. For these causes the Jews caught me in the temple, and went about to kill me.

"Having therefore obtained help of God, I continue unto this day, witnessing both to small and great, saying none other things than those which the prophets and Moses did say should come: That Christ should suffer, and that he should be the first that should rise from the dead, and should show light unto the people, and to the Gentiles."

When Paul finished speaking, Festus said with a loud voice, "Paul, you are beside yourself; much learning has made you mad."

Paul answered, "I am not mad, most noble Festus; but speak forth the words of truth and soberness. For the king knows of these things, before whom also I speak freely: for I am persuaded that none of these things are hidden from him; for this thing was not done in a corner."

Paul then turned to the king and asked, "King Agrippa, do you believe the prophets? I know that you believe."

Then Agrippa said unto Paul, "You almost persuade me to be a Christian."

Then the king, Bernice, the governor and those that sat with them rose and went out and talked among themselves, coming to the conclusion that Paul might have been set free if he had not appealed to Caesar. The decision was made: Paul would go to Rome.

The day following the hearing with the king, Philip visited Paul in prison again. The news Paul gave him filled him with mixed emotions. "I'm going to Rome, Philip! Soon we will be sailing to Italy and when we reach Rome, I will go before Nero to appeal my case."

"Do you feel like there is a chance for your release?" Philip asked anxiously.

Paul answered, "I have fought a good fight. I have kept the faith. Whether I am released or not, does not matter, for there is a crown waiting for me. The Lord told me I would go to Rome and to Rome I go, even if it is in prison clothes."

Joy Haney

"When do you sail?" asked Philip.

"Soon," Paul said. "Summer is ending. Autumn will be here and we will be going before winter. Tell Luke to get ready to travel and to bring all my things."

As Philip left the barracks he could not help feeling heavy in his spirit. He knew that it had been prophesied for Paul to go to Rome, but in chains? He felt like he might never see Paul again. It seemed so final. So many things had been happening lately. The level of persecution had seemed to increase. He had heard so much about Nero and his cruelties. He could not forsee mercy from such a wicked man.

When he reached his house he went in and sat down in a chair and just looked off into space thinking. Soon he was joined by his four daughters who asked him what was wrong. They could read on his countenance an expression of doom.

"Oh, I shouldn't be this way, but Paul is leaving to go to Rome to appeal to Caesar concerning the accusations of the Jews. Somehow I feel we will never see Paul again."

"Father!" cried Charitine. "He is such a gentle man; so wise and good."

"We will miss him greatly," chimed in Hermoine.

"Father," added Eutychiane, "I just feel like something terrible is going to happen in the near future. It has been weighing on my mind for several days now. It is not so much for us personally but for the Church at large. Whatever could it be?"

"Now girls, we must trust the Lord just as we have always done," Philip admonished them. "We will give him our fears, and pray fervently for the future of the Church. No matter what happens we must all be true and faithful to our commitment."

"Father, can we pray for the Christians in Rome, Jerusalem, and all the cities?" asked Hermoine. "I, too, feel like something awful is going to happen soon."

So it was, Philip and his family knelt once again to pray for a young Church that was growing so quickly that leaders in all major cities were beginning to take note.

Joy Haney

Chapter 12

Paul was now a prisoner on his way to Rome.

ROME. Within a circuit of little more than twelve miles more than two million people were crowded. It housed luxury and squalor, wealth and want. The handicraft employments and professions were in the hands of slaves. They cared for nothing beyond bread for the day, the games of the Circus, and the savage delight of gladiatorial shows. Manufacturing and trade were regarded as the business of the slave and foreigner. The number of slaves was about a million. The number of foreigners was much smaller, but every kind of nationality and religion found its representative in Rome.

It was the center of political and intellectual life. The rich man went to Rome to enjoy himself, the poor to beg, the new citizen to give his vote, the citizen who had been dispossessed to reclaim his rights. Rome was built on a regular plan; its streets were narrow and dirty, the houses, several stories high, were flimsily built and often tumbling down. There were many lanes and alleys but only two paved ways, the Sacra and Nova, fit for the transport of heavy carriages, in the central parts of the city.

A typical Roman believed that gods controlled every activity in the world and that paying homage to them would guarantee success or at least stave off disaster. A Roman farmer would pray to Pomona, a goddess of fruit, and Ceres, a goddess of creation and growth, for a successful harvest.

Though the Romans appeased their gods through prayer and sacrifices, their religion had little relation to moral actions, which were determined more by social or familial codes of behavior. Success, not sin, was their prime concern. They would say, "Jupiter is called Best and Greatest because he does not make us just sober or wise but healthy, rich, and prosperous."

Joy Haney

Some gods were known by several names. For example, a prayer to the goddess Diana might be addressed to, "Diana, Latonia, Juno Lucina, Trivia, Luna, or whatever you wish to be called."

While prayers were an integral part of pagan worship, most people believed that sacrifice was the truly effective way to influence the gods. In Roman temples, oxen, cows, goats, lambs, horses, bulls, rams, and even dogs were sacrificed regularly. For one special event—Caligula's coronation—160,000 cows were offered up in a three-month period.

Appearance was important to the Romans. The fashionable Roman woman began her day by dressing her hair, and that was only the beginning. She next had to "paint" her face: white on her brow and arms with chalk and white lead, red on her cheeks and lips with ochre or the lees of wine, black on her eyebrows and round the eyes with ashes or powdered antimony.

Once made up, the fashionable lady, always assisted by her slave, chose her jewels set with precious stones, and put them on one by one: a diadem on her hair, earrings in her ears, a collar or trinket round her neck, a pendent on her breast, bracelets on her wrists, rings on her fingers, and circlets on her ankles.

The people were pleasure-mad. The Roman calendar contained 159 days expressly marked as holidays, of which 93 were devoted to games given at public expense. The list does not include the many ceremonies for which the State took no responsibility and supplied no funds, but which were in much favor among the people and took place in the chapels of foreign deities whose worship was officially sanctioned and in the meeting places of the guilds and colleges.

Religion presided at the birth of every one of these Roman holidays, and was more or less inseparably bound up with each. The Romans never omitted to perform even though they had long forgotten their significance. As a result of religion being mixed with games and holidays, this required a sacrifice. So woe to the winner of the horse race in the forum. The priest sacrificed the luckless racehorse immediately after it had won the victory. Its blood was collected in two vessels, and the contents of one were straightway poured over the hearth of the Regia—the traditional palace of Numa and home of the Pontifex Maximus—while the other was sent to the vestal who kept it in reserve for the year's lustrations. As for the horse's head, which had been severed by the knife of the sacrificing priest, the dwellers by the sacred way and the inhabitants of the subura fought savagely to decide which of their respective quarters should have the honor of exhibiting on the wall of one of its buildings the trophy of the "October Horse."

When the dictators later lengthened the list of games in honor of Jupiter, Apollo, Ceres, and Cybeland of flora, they designed to raise these victories, and therewith themselves, to a more than human plane. In the combats as in the races, the underlying idea was not merely to appease the gods but to capture something of their strength, momentarily incarnate in the magistrate celebrating his triumph, in the actors of the dramas, and in the victors of the contests.

The Roman crowd reveled in the spectacles of the chariot races where everything combined to quicken their curiosity and arouse their excitement: the swarming crowd, the incredible grandeur of the settings, the perfumes and gaily-colored clothing, the sanctity of the ancient religious ceremonies, the presence of the Emperor, the obstacles to be overcome, the perils to be avoided, the prowess needed to win.

They also thronged the theaters. At one point in their history they grew so lewd that the actresses were permitted to undress entirely. Their plays became so real that there was nothing imaginary. Criminals were substituted for the actor and put to death with tortures before the eyes of the crowd. The spectators were not revolted when Prometheus was torn by the nails which pinned his palms and ankles to the cross, or seared by the claws of the bear to which he had been flung as prey. They were not sickened by such exhibitions because the ghastly butcheries of the amphitheater had long since debased their feelings and perverted their instincts.

Their thirst for violence showed itself in the gladiator shows. Bets were exchanged, and lest the result be prearranged between the fighters, an instructor stood beside them ready to give orders to excite their homicidal passion by crying, "Strike! Slug! Burn him!" and if necessary, to stimulate them by thrashing them with leather straps until the blood flowed. At every wound which the gladiators inflicted on each other, the public—trembling for its stakes—reacted with increasing excitement. If the opponent of their champion happened to totter, the gamblers could not restrain their delight and savagely chanted, "That's got him! Now he's got it!" and they thrilled with barbaric joy when he crumpled under a mortal thrust.

Sometimes the loser, stunned or wounded, had not been mortally hit, but feeling unequal to continuing the struggle, laid down his arms, stretched himself on his back and raised his left arm in a mute appeal for quarter. The right of granting this rested with the victor, but the victor renounced his claim in the presence of the Emperor, who often consulted the crowd as to their preference. When the conquered man had defended himself bravely, the crowd would wave their handkerchiefs, give the thumbs-up sign and cry, "Let him go!" If they thought he should die they would put their thumbs down and yell, "Slay him!" The Emperor calmly issued the sentence by either a thumbs-up or thumbs-down sign.

Into a society that thirsted after violence and pleasure came the fervent followers of Christ. Their doctrine was totally opposite of the Roman culture. Their meetings were often called *agape,* which in Greek means "love." They constantly assisted each other without parade or patronage. An unceasing interchange of counsel, information, and practical help took place between one Christian and the other. This was alive and active in a fashion wholly different from that of the pagan brotherhoods. Many observers took note of them and said, "How simple and pure is their religion! What confidence they have in their God and his promise! How they love one another and how happy they are together."

The new Christians gave themselves to the things of the Spirit. Their lives revolved around their new experience in Christ. Prayer was a daily practice. They fasted often until their minds were prepared to believe God for anything. Miracles were common among them. They affected their world; it did not affect them.

Corruption, wickedness, violence, murder, hate, false accusations, arrogant governors, spiteful Jews, the Caesars—nothing could stop the growing Church. They fervently spread their doctrine everywhere they went. It made its way into Caesar's household, the barracks, theaters, shops, highways and cities. Paul, one of its greatest leaders, may have been a prisoner, but the gospel was not in prison. It was free, bound to no man, creed, system, or building!

60 A.D.

After a rough journey at sea Paul finally arrived on the shores of Italy and started on his journey to Rome. In several places along the way he was greeted by his friends and Christian brothers and sisters. At a place called the Three Taverns, where a crossroad from the coast at Antium came in from the left, another party of Christians was waiting to welcome and to honor the ambassador in bonds. With a lighter heart, and a more cheerful countenance, he traveled the remaining seventeen miles, which brought him along the base of the Alban Hills, to the city of Aricia. The town was above the road; on the hillside swarms of beggars met travelers as they passed. On this summit, Paul obtained his first view of Rome.

As they went along and entered into Rome the houses grew closer together. Passing under the arch Porta Capena, which was dripping with the water of the aqueduct that went over it, Julius and his prisoners moved on toward the house of Caesar. Here the household troops were quartered in a praetorium attached to the palace. Here it was that Julius gave up his prisoner to Burrus, the Praetorian Praefect, whose official duty it was to keep in custody all accused persons who were to be tried before the Emperor.

Paul remained in his own hired house; Burrus permitted him to reside there instead of confining him within the walls of the Praetorian barrack. He was still a prisoner under custody, chained by the arm both day and night to one of the Imperial bodyguards and thus subjected to the rudeness of an insolent soldiery, but he received every indulgence which was in the power of the Praefect to grant. He was allowed to receive all who came to him, and was permitted, without hindrance, to preach boldly the kingdom of God and to teach the things of the Lord Jesus Christ.

Paul's trial was temporarily suspended as the Roman courts required the personal presence of the prosecutor. His accusers had not arrived from Palestine and would not come until A.D. 61. Even after they arrived in August, the first stage of the trial would not commence until A.D. 62. During the delay of his trial, Paul resided in a house of sufficient size to accommodate the congregation which flocked together to listen to his teaching. His speech became much more eloquent with the clanking of the chain and the upraising of his fettered hand. Tears were often in the eyes of his listeners as he preached with fervor. Though he was tied to one spot, he kept up a constant interchange between other Christians who also became messengers of the gospel. Through them the Church grew rapidly.

Joy Haney

Finally the day arrived for Paul's appearance before the Emperor. In the Imperial Palace, lined with the precious marbles of Egypt and Libya, sat the Caesar with his councilors, twenty in number, men of the highest rank and greatest influence. In spite of the cruelty of Nero and his licentious living, the trial resulted in the acquittal of Paul. He was pronounced guiltless of the charges brought against him, his fetters were struck off, and he was liberated from his lengthened captivity in A.D. 63.

He wasted no time. Immediately he traveled eastward through Macedonia, ministering to the churches in Asia Minor. He traveled onward to Spain in the year 64, where he remained for about two years establishing churches along the Spanish coast. In 66 Paul returned to Ephesus from Spain, but he did not remain there long. He went first to Macedonia, and afterwards to Crete; and immediately on his return from thence, he left Ephesus for Rome, by way of Corinth.

Chapter 13

BACK TO A.D. 64

The tolerant attitude of Nero's government towards Christianity was suddenly transformed into cruel hostility. In July a great fire broke out in Rome which raged for nine days; out of fourteen civic districts, three were totally destroyed, seven partially. Although Nero was at Antium when the fire broke out, it was suspected that he instigated or deliberately had the fire started.

The common belief in Nero's guilt, and the danger of revolution—owing to bitterness engendered in many thousands of ruined and homeless sufferers—led to the accusation placed against the Christians. Nero sought to put blame on the Christians and said that they tried to burn the pagan temples because of their hostility to society and by their expectation of an impending destruction of the world by fire.

The most brutal persecution against Christians increased greatly at this time in Rome and other cities governed by Rome. Some were nailed to crosses; others were sewn up in the skins of wild beasts and exposed to the fury of wild dogs; others again were smeared over with combustible materials and were used as torches to illuminate the darkness of the night. The gardens of Nero were often lit with flaming Christians placed on poles, and while he played the lyre and sang songs the Christians burned.

In a dimly lit room in the east wing of the palace where Nero ruled as Emperor, several slaves of the Imperial household gathered together. Amplias, the leader, talked to them about the growing unrest and false accusations that were rising rapidly against the Christians.

"It has been thirty years now since I have been a Christian. Since my conversion, I have seen thousands converted to the truth of Jesus' doctrine. Even now Caesar's household is full of Christians, and I fear for their lives.

"When Nero first became Emperor he showed tolerance towards us, but now he has become like a cruel animal that bares his teeth and hisses at his enemy. Even now, some of our fellow Christians have been eaten alive in the arena by wild beasts and some have been crucified.

"It is my prayer," continued Amplias, "that you will stand strong and be not afraid. Whatever happens, stay true to the doctrines of Christ."

As they were talking and encouraging one another, there came a knock at the door. Immediately fear gripped them. A deathlike quiet pervaded the room and then the door opened. One of Nero's trusted servants entered with an evil smile, pointed to two members of the group, Stachy and Nereus, and said, "You are wanted by the Emperor, now!"

Stachy and Nereus looked from face to face as if to memorize each one's features; then as the henchman prodded them they saluted their fellow workers and left as the guard leered at the others in the group.

When the two were brought before Nero, he jeeringly told them he had proof that they had helped start the fire which burned much of the city.

"You will die tomorrow for the crime you have committed!" he raged.

They were thrust out of Nero's presence and were half pushed, half dragged down the long hall toward the dungeon where they would stay the long, dark night. As the bars clanged shut behind the two men, they fell to the ground and prayed to God that he would be with them. They remembered what the Apostle had instructed them to do: "Count it all joy when you are called upon to be persecuted for Christ's sake." They prayed until peace filled their hearts and then they settled down for the night, knowing that all was well.

Early the next morning the guards threw open the door to the dungeon and led the two men into an open chamber where they were thrown on a table and tied up by merciless men. Next they were encased in the skins of wild beasts which had been freshly killed. The blood smeared their faces and hands as one of Nero's men took a large needle used for tentmaking and sewed Stachy and Nereus inside the skins. They were totally encased in blood, maggots, and rotting flesh that still clung to the hides.

Next they felt themselves thrown onto the back of an open carriage which they knew led away to the arena—the dreaded place they had discussed with the group yesterday. They felt the carriage slow down as they neared the arena. Rough men picked them up like sacks of potatoes and threw them onto the floor of one of the side rooms. As they felt the impact of the fall they heard the roar of the blood-thirsty crowd.

Stachy said weakly, "Nereus, let us be strong in the end. This is not the end; it is only the beginning. We are going home to be with the Lord. No matter what pain you feel, remember it is a victory, not a defeat."

Nereus answered, "No matter what is done to us, they cannot stop the Church. The gospel of Jesus Christ is spreading everywhere and our bloodshed will only increase the fervor of our fellow Christians. Persecution, bloodshed, or demon power will never win over this Church!"

Then the inner doors were flung open with a loud clang and the two men sewn in animal skins were carelessly picked up and cast on a litter carried by four men. The four advanced to the center of the arena, tossed their burden off and retreated behind locked doors as they heard the roar of the hungry wild dogs about to be loosed upon them.

At the report of the cannon the wild dogs came barking towards the blood-smeared objects. Nereus and Stachy felt the saliva drip as the dogs' teeth begin to maul them. The tearing, ripping, and mauling caused such excruciating pain that they each prayed for death to overtake them. At last, what was left of them lay in pieces on a bloodstained floor.

The courage of the martyrs gave others strength to continue. As the martyrs' blood darkened the earth, more glorious grew the Church! Revival fires burned, miracles increased, prayer and fasting became as natural as breathing, while the Word grew steadily in power among them.

The bishop of Antioch summed up all their sentiments: "Come fire, come cross; grapplings with wild beasts, cuttings and manglings, wrenching of bones, hacking of limbs, crushing of the whole body; let cruel torments of the devil come upon me; if only I may attain unto Jesus Christ." With fervent appeal such as this, Christians everywhere embraced their martyrdom. Their chains were considered only as "spiritual pearls."

Meanwhile in A.D. 65, the revolt which developed into the great Jewish war broke out at Caesarea. Philip, with his four daughters, left the city and settled at Tralles in Asia Minor. There he performed many miracles and was instrumental in building up the Church in that city, eventually becoming its leader.

Chapter 14

A.D. 66

The Church in Rome enjoyed such phenomenal growth, in spite of the persecutions, that it incited fear and jealousy in the hearts of the governmental leaders. Because of this growth, Nero had made a new law which prohibited the propagation of a new and illicit religion among the citizens of Rome. Nero's attention was drawn to Paul because a young woman that was one of his mistresses was converted by Paul's preaching. She stopped the lewd course of life she had been living, and Nero became incensed. He had Paul arrested, but this time he was treated as a common criminal without any special privileges. He was not only chained, but treated as a malefactor.

A.D. 68

Two important figures met their deaths in 68: Paul, the Apostle, and Nero, the Emperor. Paul, who had arrived in Rome and had been in the Mammerton Prison for about two years, was on Nero's death list. Paul knew the time of his death[5] was soon, for he wrote to Timothy a letter concerning it. He said,

For I am now ready to be offered, and the time of my departure is at hand. I have fought a good fight, I have finished my course, I have kept the faith: Henceforth there is laid up for me a crown of righteousness, which the Lord, the righteous judge, shall give me at that day: and not to me only, but unto all them also that love his

---

[5] The privileges of Roman citizenship exempted Paul from the death of lingering torture, which had been lately inflicted on so many of his brethren. He was to die by decapitation. The constitutional mode of inflicting capital punishment on a Roman citizen was by the lictor's axe. The criminal was tied to a stake; cruelly scourged with rods, and then beheaded. But the military mode of execution—decapitation by the sword—was more usual under Nero.

appearing. Do your diligence to come shortly unto me: For Demas has forsaken me, having loved this present world. Only Luke is with me. The cloak that I left at Troas with Carpus, when you come, bring with you, and the books, but especially the parchments. Do your diligence to come before winter.

Love,
Paul

It was a hot summer day when Nero, in one of his moods, decided that Paul should die. The guards came and treated Paul roughly, shoving and pushing the elderly Apostle who had impacted the world. The door of the prison clang shut behind Paul for the last time. As the martyr began his death march toward the cruel, mocking executioner, the world outside continued to go and come between the metropolis and its harbor: Merchants hastening to superintend the unloading of their cargoes, sailors eager to squander the profits of their last voyage in the allurements of the capital, officials of the government busy with the administration of the Provinces, Chaldean astrologers seeing into the future, dancing-girls from Syria performing with their painted turbans, priests performing sacrifices,

Greek adventurers eager to coin their talent into Roman gold, the fraud, the lust, the superstition and intelligence. Through the dust and tumult of the busy throng, the small troop of soldiers threaded their way under the bright sky of an Italian midsummer with Paul as their prisoner.

Paul the Apostle, Prophet, and now the martyr, poured forth his blood for the greatest cause on earth: the cause of Jesus Christ, the Lord! Weeping friends took up his corpse and carried it to the Catacombs for burial where the persecuted Church found refuge for the living, and sepulchers for the dead.

So it was that the martyrdom of Paul and the other Christians became the means whereby revival flooded all the then-known world until, as Paul said, "every creature under heaven" had the gospel preached unto them.

Epilogue

A.D. 325

The following is a letter from one descendant of Philip to another.

Dear Julia,

Have you heard the latest news out of Rome? Everyone here is talking about the Council of Nicaea. The Emperor Constantine has brought peace to the Roman Church. There has not been any persecutions for quite some time now, but a noticeable change has been taking place in many of the established churches.

The biggest news is that the original baptism of the early Church has been changed. They did away with the immersion in the water and now are sprinkling their converts. They also changed the formula for baptism. Instead of proclaiming in the name of Jesus, they are substituting the titles, "In the Father, Son, and Holy Ghost."

What do you think Philip would think about this? What about the Apostle Paul? You know all the stories handed down to us from generation to generation, of how so many of the early followers of Christ were persecuted because of the new doctrine of salvation and baptism—do you think they died in vain? Or do you think there are those who are going to continue baptizing like the original Church did in the Book of The Acts of the Apostles?

We have discussed it in our household and we have decided to continue baptizing as Paul baptized when he was in Corinth, as told in Acts 19. Remember when he found some disciples there and he asked them how they were baptized and if they had received the Holy Ghost? And they said they had never heard of the Holy Ghost, and they had been baptized according to John's baptism?

My husband said to me, "As Paul instructed them, we are going to continue in his doctrine."

I must say goodbye for now. Give all your family my love. I miss you so—it will be a joy to me when I see you again.

God bless you.

Love,
Aunt Priscilla

Joy Haney

Additional References on Baptism

The following references from encyclopedias, Bible dictionaries, and religious history books will help give clearer understanding of the original mode of baptism.

An Encyclopedia of Religions, by Maurice Canney, p. 53:

Persons were baptized at first "In the name of Jesus Christ" (Acts 2:38, 10:48) or "In the name of the Lord Jesus" (Acts 8:16, 19:5). Afterwards with the development of the doctrine of the Trinity, they were baptized "In the name of the Father and of the Son and of the Holy Ghost."

Encyclopedia of Religion and Ethics, by James Hastings, Vol. 2, pp. 378-9:

p. 378...whereupon the latter sealed the reception of the candidate into the holy community by invoking "the fair name" of the Lord Jesus upon his head.

p. 389...The earliest known formula is "in the name of the Lord Jesus" or some similar phrase...

Interpreter's Dictionary of the Bible, 1962 Edition, Vol. 1, p. 351:

The evidence of Acts 2:38; 10:48; (ch. 8:16; 19:5), supported by Gal. 3:27; Rom. 6:3, suggests that baptism in early Christianity was administered not in the threefold name, but "in the name of Jesus Christ" or "in the name of the Lord Jesus."

Joy Haney

A Dictionary of the Bible, by James Hastings, Vol. 1, p. 241:

The original form of words was "into the name of Jesus Christ" or "the Lord Jesus." Baptism into the name of the Trinity was a later development.

The New Schaff-Herzog Encyclopedia of Religious Knowledge, 1966 Edition, Vol. 1, pp. 435-6:

p. 435...the New Testament knows only baptism in the name of Jesus (Acts 2:38; 8:16; 19:5; Gal. 3:27; Rom. 6:3; I Cor. 1:13-15), which still occurs even in the second and third centuries, while the Trinitarian formula occurs only in Matt. 28:19;...It is unthinkable that the Apostolic Church thus obeyed the express command of the Lord, which it otherwise considered the highest authority.

p. 436...The Greek phrase "baptize in or into the name Jesus" means the act of baptism takes place with the utterance of the name of Jesus.

Scribner's Encyclopedia of Religion and Ethics, Vol. 1, p. 380:

Christian baptism, when connected with the mention of a formula, is alluded to four times in the Acts (2:38; 8:16; 10:48; 19;5) and the formula is never that of (Matt. 28:19) but is twice in the name of Jesus Christ (Acts 2:38; Acts 10:48). And twice into the name of the Lord Jesus (Acts 8:16; 19:5). That this was the usual formula of Christian baptism is supported by the evidence of the Pauline Epistles, which speak of being baptized only into Christ or into Christ Jesus (Gal. 3:27; Rom. 6:3). Is it possible to reconcile these facts with the belief that Christ commanded the disciples to baptize in the triune name? The obvious explanation of the silence of NT. on the triune name, and the use of another formula in Acts and Paul is that this other formula was the earlier, and that the triune formula is a later edition. It would require very strong argument to controvert this presumption, and none seems to exist.

Christianity in the Apostolic Age, by George Gilbert, p. 25:

Baptism into the name of Jesus is the only form mentioned in the book of Acts and the New Testament epistles.

Dictionary of the Bible, edited by James Hastings, 1963 Revised Edition, p. 88:

...the primitive Church baptized "in" or "into the name of Jesus" (or "Jesus Christ," or "the Lord Jesus" (I Cor. 1:13, 15; Acts 8:16; 19:5)...Thus the spoken formula, "in the name of Jesus," effected the presence of the risen Lord and gave the baptized into His possession and protection.

The Religious Experience of the Primitive Church, 1937 Edition, pp. 31, 282:

p. 31...In the primitive community the rite marked the admission of the new convert who in the very reception of the baptism was aware of his surrender made to, and accepted by Jesus the Lord whom he confessed and whose name was pronounced over him.

p. 282...Those who pronounce the name of Jesus over the person receiving baptism are acting for the real purchaser, Jesus Christ, whose name has a virtue able to possess and protect the one over whom his name is pronounced.

Sources Consulted

After Jesus, The Triumph of Christianity. Pleasantville, N.Y.: Reader's Digest, n.d.

Carcopino, Jerome. *Daily Life in Ancient Rome.* New Haven and London: Yale University Press, 1940.

Coleman, William. *Today's Handbook of Bible Times and Customs.* Minneapolis: Bethany House Publishers, 1984.

Conybeare, W.J., J.S. Howson. *The Life, Times and Travels of St. Paul.* New York: E.B. Treat & Co., 1869.

Encyclopedia Britannica, Volume 6, Chicago, Illinois, 1942

Fox's Book of Martyrs. Philadelphia: Henry T. Coates & Co., n.d.

Gibbon, Edward. *The Decline and Fall of the Roman Empire.* New York: Washington Square Press, 1960.

Hastings, James. *A Dictionary of the Bible.* Edinburgh: T & T Clark, 1910.

Henry, Matthew. *Matthew Henry's Commentary on the Whole Bible.* London: Fisher, 1845.

Josephus, Flavius. *The Complete Works of Josephus.* Grand Rapids Michigan: Kregel Publications, 1960.

Lockyer, Herbert. *Women of the Bible.* Grand Rapids, Michigan: Zondervan, 1967.

Joy Haney